Blackhawk Recollections

Blackhawk Recollections

86th Infantry Division Members Remember

Compiled and edited by
Austin "Red" Goodrich

iUniverse, Inc.
New York Bloomington Shanghai

Blackhawk Recollections
86th Infantry Division Members Remember

Copyright © 2008 by Austin Goodrich

All rights reserved. No part of this book may be used or reproduced by any means, graphic, electronic, or mechanical, including photocopying, recording, taping or by any information storage retrieval system without the written permission of the publisher except in the case of brief quotations embodied in critical articles and reviews.

iUniverse books may be ordered through booksellers or by contacting:

iUniverse
1663 Liberty Drive
Bloomington, IN 47403
www.iuniverse.com
1-800-Authors (1-800-288-4677)

Because of the dynamic nature of the Internet, any Web addresses or links contained in this book may have changed since publication and may no longer be valid.

The views expressed in this work are solely those of the author and do not necessarily reflect the views of the publisher, and the publisher hereby disclaims any responsibility for them.

ISBN: 978-0-595-49556-6 (pbk)
ISBN: 978-0-595-61149-2 (ebk)

Printed in the United States of America

Contents

PREFACE vii
    SALUTE TO THE 86TH BLACKHAWK DIVISION MEMORIAL ix
    WHY SUPPORT A BLACKHAWK MEMORIAL? xi

PART ONE: CIVILIAN SOLDIERS 1
    GENESIS 3
    THE RE-HUMANIZATION OF ED WANDTKE 6
    SURVIVOR'S GUILT 8
    HOW ASTP BASIC TRAINING BROUGHT LOVE, HAPPINESS 11
    LIFE CHANGERS: ASTP AND THE GI BILL 12
    A TRIBUTE TO THE ASTP WHIZ KIDS 13
    FRANK CAMPANA....BLACKHAWK'S GIFT TO SHOW BIZ 14
    THE BLACKHAWK COMMANDOS 15
    21ST REUNION MEMORIAL ADDRESS 17

PART TWO: EUROPEAN THEATER 23
    A BREATHLESS PASSAGE 25
    MEMOIRS OF A BAZOOKA MAN 28
    THE DAY THE WAR GOT REAL 30
    CAPTAIN MAC AND ME 33
    A SLICE OF COMBAT … AND BALONEY 37
    TEXAS BAR-B-Q: AUSTRIAN STYLE 38
    SAVING OUR OWN "PVT. RYAN" 40
    RECOLLECTION OF A GRAVEL-CLUTCHER* 41
    HOW WAYNE MICKIE MARTIN FOUGHT THE WAR! 44

HIGHLIGHTS OF MY POSTWAR LIFE: 53
CROSSING MY RUBICON 55
HOW I SKIPPED THE PACIFIC THEATER 62
THE BEST JOB IN THE ARMY I 64
MY BUDDY—GENERAL POPE 69
THE BEST PEA SOUP EVER 72
BLACKHAWK TWINS I 73
BLACKHAWK TWINS II 75
A LONG AND WINDING ROAD 76
A DAY IN THE RUHR REMEMBERED 77
I REMEMBER AL JOSLYN, PRIVATE FOR LIFE 78
APPLE ASS VOGEL, M.D. 79
BLACKHAWK DUTY, A FAMILY TRADITION 81
THE 86TH BLACKHAWK DIVISION MEMORIAL HIGHWAY 82
REUNION GUEST SPEAKER: SOLDIER BOB DOLE 83
HOW WE ALMOST DESTROYED THE SOUND OF MUSIC 85
RANDOM BLACKHAWK MUSINGS 86
RECOLLECTIONS OF WAR 93
COMBAT: UP CLOSE AND PERSONAL 95
COLLATERAL DAMAGE 96

PART THREE: FINALE 99
FRANK BURNS: AN EARLY BLACKHAWK BUSINESSMAN 101
A STAR WAS BORN … IN MANILA 1945 103
ONE DOWN, ONE TO GO 105
A GOOD PEOPLE LOYAL AND INDUSTRIOUS 106
BLACKHAWKS SALUTE OUR FLAG 108
MINDANAO MISSION 109
HOW I NEARLY BECAME THE MAIN COURSE 112
THE LAST BATTLE 114
A NECESSARY DETOUR 115

PREFACE

As the 86th Blackhawk Infantry Division Association prepares to fade into the hallowed past of our nation's history, we decided to publish a collection of our members' experiences during World War II. It is our fond hope that these memoirs, as varied as the personalities and backgrounds of their writers, will produce in future generations a deeper understanding and appreciation of what was done to gain the final victory. There has been minimal effort to organize these highly subjective recollections chronologically or topically, and if this produces in the reader a sense of disorder and confusion then we will have succeeded in depicting war exactly as we experienced it with apologies to no one who might want history to be put through a critical mangle iron to smooth out the wrinkles produced by the humanoid critters who fashioned it. Welcome, dear readers, to the real world of conflict in its most cruel and demanding, stimulating, depressing and uplifting—that is to say—in its most human form.

SALUTE TO THE 86TH BLACKHAWK DIVISION MEMORIAL

All profits derived from the sale of this book will be used to pay for the erection and maintenance of the 86th Blackhawk Infantry Division Memorial at Camp San Luis Obispo, CA. Please mail tax deductible donations to: Operation Blackhawk Memorial, 370 Glenallyn Dr., Valparaiso, IN 46383. Thank you!

Blackhawk Association Board 2008 left to right: Larry Bennett, Austin Goodrich, Gene Lowe, Frank Potter, Dave Herold, Jerry Deitz and Dick Behrends.

WHY SUPPORT A BLACKHAWK MEMORIAL?

by Bob Rasmus, 342 L Co

All my life, as I have visited different parts of America, I have seen memorials erected to honor those who gave their lives in our nation's wars. I have always been touched by the sentiments expressed on those monuments—feelings of respect, of gratitude, of sorrow. I believe we surviving members of the 86th Division have a great opportunity to create a memorial for our own comrades who died in our war.

Our memorial would be blessed by several advantages. The first is that the bronze infantryman surmounting the monument would be sculpted by a gifted member of our division. The artist being one of our own would undoubtedly make it unique among the memorials of any military unit. Locating it at Camp San Luis Obispo, where we received our final training, would be ideal. And it's in a part of America that attracts many visitors because of its scenic beauty. Finally, the memorial would be in protected surroundings because the base will, for the foreseeable future, be in use by the National Guard, security training organizations and a technology college. Creating this memorial is something we should do, mainly for four groups of people:

For our comrades—our buddies—who gave their lives in the war. Surely we owe them this remembrance.

For their surviving families and descendants. In the recent Ken Burns' documentary, "The War", I was struck by the fresh grief, even after more than sixty years, of the siblings and other family members of the people who died in that war. I think of the first two men who died in our company, Earl Roat and Robert Johns, both leaving wives carrying their unborn children. I can imagine the pride of these offspring, now in their sixties, upon seeing their father's names on that memorial.

For our buddies who survived the war, but have died since. Surely their families and descendants would take pride in seeing a monument depicting the Blackhawk's role in the war.

And, finally, for our own families when we are gone.

Note: The stories in this book first appeared in the 86th Blackhawk Division Association newsletter, The Bugle. Requests for permission to reprint any of them in whole or in part should be directed to the publisher: iUniverse, 2021 Pine Lake Rd., Suite 100, Lincoln, NE 68512. Via internet: www.iuniverse.com or telephone: 1–800–288–4677.

PART ONE

CIVILIAN SOLDIERS

August 1917: 86th Division activated at Camp Grant, IL

January 1943: Reactivated at Camp Howze, TX, moved to Camp Livingston, LA and Camp San Luis Obispo, CA before deployment to the European Theatre of Operations.

GENESIS

From the very beginning, the 86th Blackhawk Infantry Division of the United States Army was an anomaly. Originally established as a reserve division in World War I, it was comprised mainly of conscripts from Illinois and Wisconsin. The outfit was named after a famous military leader of the Sauk Indian tribe known as Black Hawk. Because the unit's insignia—a black hawk on a red shield—closely resembled the Prussian eagle that adorned German army helmets, the letters B and H were added. The division with the suspiciously Teutonic emblem was sent to France, but never fought as a unit because its troops were assigned as replacements for casualties in line units. Perhaps the name became best known as the designation of the Chicago Blackhawks professional hockey team, whose owner Frederic McLaughlin served in the division in WWI.

The division was reactivated at Camp Howze, Texas, in December, 1942. Many of its troops were deployed to the European Theater of Operations (ETO) and were replaced by college-bound ASTP soldiers and Air Force cadets when the division was re-located in late 1943 to Camp Livingston, Louisiana. This gave rise to a staffing situation that turned Plato's prescription for an ideal society upside down, with the more intelligent, better educated citizens at the bottom and the less-educated, libido-driven members of society in command.

A recipe for disaster? Not at all. By virtue of some sort of weird alchemy, the Blackhawk societal mixture worked. Mutual distrust was somehow transformed into a pervasive climate of trust and admiration that led to the bonding of the most disparate of cultural and educational backgrounds into a unified, smoothly functioning whole. A worm's eye view of life at the bottom of the 86th Division's Table of Organization may help explain the human dynamics at work in this curious amalgam.

The officers and non-coms at the upper levels of the power pyramid at Camp Livingston initially viewed those of us who came from the ASTP basic training program at Fort Benning with distaste bordering on contempt. We were collectively designated as the FBI, an acronym for Fort Benning Idiots. Our response was to demonstrate by word and deed that we youngsters (most of us were eighteen years old) were at least the equal of the over-thirty, cigarette freaks with beer bellies who outranked us. The new-found pride that united us in our struggle to gain the respect of our nominal superiors accompanied our assignment to a line infantry division. We were no longer "casuals," pieces of meat to be processed, stripped of our identity and human dignity, homeless, without status or respect. To avoid the casual label, wounded GIs have been known to straggle along behind their units. If sent to a hospital they escaped to rejoin their units to avoid ending up in a replacement center as casuals.

Although some of our comrades were less than delighted to be assigned to the infantry, we were all happy to have a permanent home. We were proud to wear a cap with the infantry blue piping and a hawkish division shoulder patch on our shirts and jackets. As important as they were to our self-esteem, these physical signs of membership were insufficient proof of our belonging to a line division. We had to win our claim to a permanent identity first of all in the eyes of our superiors.

The non-coms did their best to wear us down and out with calisthenics. It was standard procedure for a non-com to lead the drill by counting cadence as he performed the exercises along with his young charges. Instead, it was the non-com who had to be relieved by one of his peers. This produced disparaging remarks from the ranks about flabby beer bellies and overage sergeants. When other noncoms, who prowled the outskirts of the group heard these remarks, they ordered the miscreants to go through punishment drill. This consisted of running around the perimeter of the parade ground with rifle raised overhead in a painful position. It was customary for a non-com to run alongside the victim, goading him to keep up his speed. Contrary to his plan, the non-com often fell behind and was goaded by his charge to keep pace.

Having won respect for our physical capabilities we had to gain respect for our minds and our right to express ourselves as free-thinking, if obedient, members of our nation's civilian army. One astute spokesman was PFC Lothrop Mittenthal (342nd K Co), who had become a cadet colonel of all high school ROTC units in Los Angeles by memorizing Army field manuals. One Saturday afternoon, a pimply-faced 90-day wonder delivered a stumbling lecture on the need for self reliance in the infantry private. Upon seeing his superior officers enter the room, and seeking to make a favorable impression, the lieutenant pointed to an apparently dozing Mittenthal and said: "You there in the front row, what do *you* think the attributes of an infantry private should be?" Lothrop replied immediately: "I think that all infantry privates should be apes." The young officer shot back, "Why?"

"An ape can do everything that I can do," said Lothrop, "and besides that, he has a tail and can swing through the trees and I can't do that."

Nonplussed, the lieutenant blurted out: Well, what about the officers and non-commissioned officers?"

Lothrop responded, "Oh, leave them as they are. They're only a little better than apes anyway!" Fortunately, this exchange struck the two senior officers as hilariously funny and there were no repercussions.

Mittenthal's outspoken irreverence for rank was expressed eagerly one morning in a confrontation with squad leader Sgt. Victor Renda, an Italo-American from Des Moines. Although as a civilian, Renda had nothing but contempt for men who helped their wives with the housework, he had become a neat-freak in the Army. Every morning he wakened his charges with the exhortation: "All right, snap shit, let's get this place cleaned up!" Generally he was forced to overcome his sluggish subordinates' inertia by sweeping out the hut by himself. But one morning the daily snap shit command caused Mittenthal to fix his superior with his baleful, bespectacled eyes and observe: "Sergeant Renda, you are a red-assed baboon." Renda jumped back with a startled expression but said nothing. Later in the day, he asked me in private "What is wrong with that guy? Is he crazy or something?" I replied, Yeah, you gotta watch him. He's a math major at Cal Tech."

The Fort Benning Idiots were admittedly a mixed bag of iconoclasts, most of whom were deeply dedicated to serve our country's military needs while reserving the right to question its hierarchical system. A Latin scholar among us noted that *private* is derived from a word meaning not only "belongs to ones self" but also "set apart from the state, deprived of office." In our literal application of this definition, which provided us with more flexibility in the decision-making area than exists in most armies, the privates of the Blackhawk Division presented a united front—with at least one notable exception, Ed Wandtke, who will serve as an example of the pre-combat phase of our Blackhawk experience.

The Re-humanization of Ed Wandtke
by Austin "Red" Goodrich 342 K Co.

Ed's grandfather had been an *Uhlan* (lancer) in the Prussian Army and some of this military allegiance had been squeezed down through two generations. Unlike most of us, Ed actually liked the army life and planned to make a career of it after the war. This plan was viewed as sheer lunacy by his comrades, even though two of Ed's platoon mates did re-up during the Koran war, but as commissioned officers. The aforementioned Lothrop Mittenthal was one. The other was John List, who in 1971 shot and killed his mother, wife and three teenage children. None of his Blackhawk Division comrades could believe that this gentle peson could ever commit such a crime. An explanation appeared in 2001 while he was serving a five consecutive life terms sentence in a New Jersey prison: John List was officially diagnosed as suffering from Post Traumatic Stress Disorder incurred during the war.

Regardless of how Ed Wandke had come by *his* damaged genes, his platoon mates agreed unanimously that early intensive therapy would be needed to cure his disorder. Otherwise, Ed's deranged attitude might undermine the unity and morale of the platoon and, worse, offer encouragement to our officers and non-com oppressors.

The educational process began one evening at 1900 Hours when Ed retired, saying he had a headache and would we please leave the hut so he could get some shuteye. About twenty minutes later a voice yelled in the door, "Get up, Ed, Sgt Ramsey wants to see you!" Platoon Sgt. Ramsey was Regular Army, a West Virginia mountain man who knew how to bank the coals in our pot-bellied stove at night to break through at exactly five the next morning. He also knew how to strip his troops of their meager paychecks in "friendly" poker games played with his deck of cards on top of his footlocker on paydays.

Just such a game was in progress when Ed appeared at the door of his hut dressed in Class-A uniform, including necktie. Ramsey looked up from his cards just long enough to rumble "Naw, I don't wanna see you. Git outta here."

Fifteen minutes later another voice called out to Ed. "Go to the Day Room, Wandke. You gotta make up a class in chemical warfare." Burned once, Ed went back to sleep. Ten minutes later an angry lieutenant appeared at the door and demanded to know in a loud voice why Ed had refused to obey orders. Ed ran to the Day Room where he spent an hour listening to fatuous information on CW, after which he staggered back to his bunk.

About 20 minutes later, three of Pfc Wandtke's comrades rousted him to obey an order to accompany them on a walk to the ordnance repair shop to pick up a mortar. Although a 60 mm mortar weighed only forty pounds and could easily be carried by one man, Wandtke was not one to argue that his presence on the detail was unneeded. After all, orders are orders, and Ed was not about to go against a major tenet of his military philosophy.

When we arrived at the ordnance depot it was closed and we started to walk a mile and a half back to our K Company huts in the dead of night. About half way back, Ed suddenly began to lurch about, moaning and groaning. Then he suddenly lay down in the middle of the road and began to cry. His headache by then had reached Vesuvian heights and all of the injustices of military life suddenly closed in on him. Pfc Wandtke swore a great oath to the effect that from day forward he would be the world champ opponent of the Army.

His re-humanizing education was complete and all of Ed's buddies welcomed his return to normalcy as a most positive development. Henceforth we privates could present a solid phalanx to the powers that were. Even the officers and non-coms were pleased, as they could now understand Ed's world view.

Survivor's Guilt
by Alfred "Ted" Goodwin, 342nd 3rd Bn Hqs Co

"Ted" Goodwin

In September of 1944, following the levy of both officers and EM to overseas replacement assignments in response to losses during the invasion of Normandy, and heavy casualties in the Pacific, the division at Camp Livingston, LA, received a significant number of ASTP enlisted men and new officers from Ft. Benning. About the same time, the still depleted enlisted and junior officer ranks were brought up to Table of Organization strength by "retreads" from the air force, the coast artillery, and other sources, to be retrained by the 86th Division for amphibious operations in the Pacific.

Most of the new "ninety day wonders" were third year ROTC students who were still in training at Benning when 1944's heavy casualties were sustained overseas. My ROTC (Oregon) class of 1944, in peace time, would have been commissioned on the campus. Instead, we were mobilized in 1942, trained as infantrymen in 1943, and commissioned at OCS during stateside duty. These young officers were just a year or two older than the ASTP trainees who joined them as rookie Blackhawks during the fall of 1944. The 342nd Infantry that boarded the *Kungsholm* bound for Le Havre carried a lot of college kids in enlisted grades one and two, and a lot of shiny new gold bars on lieutenants fresh from ROTC and Fort Benning. The senior noncoms and company commanders, since Camp Howze, had been hand picked for retention during the repeated levies for replacements. The division was a good cross section of what Tom Brokaw later called "The Greatest Generation."

While we were still at Camp Livingston, Maj. Ward saw me in the I Co. area, sitting outside my hut with a portable typewriter, banging away on a letter home. He was in his jeep, with T/5 Vernon Moore driving, and stopped. I jumped up and saluted. He said, "Goodwin can you type?" I said "Yes, Sir!" The next thing I knew, he had me transferred from I Co., where First Sgt. Stafford was training me, over to 3rd. Bn. HQ Co. There I was assigned, on paper, to the Ammunition and Pioneer Platoon, and in fact, to a pile of army forms and a GI typewriter. Concurrent training as a powder monkey and as a clerk-typist filled the remaining days at Livingston. Assisting a gung-ho West Pointer with his paper work, which he hated, was fun but stressful. In the field, or later, with the Navy on amphibious training, life was strictly demolition ammunition supply. When in garrison long enough to change clothes, it was the life of a "ball-bearing WAAC," typing up the major's reports. In 1990, at a high school class reunion, I told my typing teacher that she probably saved my life in Germany. Instead of leading a rifle platoon in marching fire, like my ROTC classmates, I was further back in the column, herding ammunition deuce and a halfs as calls came in for more mortar ammo and boxes of machine gun belts.

Sixty years later, I still carry a burden of survivor's guilt. The lieutenant who took my place in I Company was killed in the German mortar barrage that greeted the first platoon's crossing of the Danube. Lt. John Seaton was a class of '44 ROTC student from the University of Montana. Whenever someone brings up World War II, I think of John, the Big Sky he never got to see again, and of the random craziness of assignments and deployments when a nation goes to war.

How ASTP Basic Training Brought Love, Happiness
by Denton Harris, 342nd 3rdBn Hqs Co.

In the Christmas season of 1943, the pastor of a large Atlanta church knew our lieutenant at Ft.Benning and asked him to bring some ASTP trainees to his church. I was one of the lucky ones. We stayed at the Bentley Hotel ("Room and Bath for a dollar and a half"). Three of us were invited by a church member to Sunday dinner. Their 15-year-old daughter asked two neighbor girls to join us. My wife, then 14, was one of them.

Four years later I caught a free ride with my college professor who lived at Highlands, NC. That 14-year-old girl had grown up (and so had I!) I realized that she was "the one" even though my girl friend back home became "Miss Southeastern Arkansas." A year later we were married. That was 57 years ago before two daughters and six wonderful grandchildren arrived to make us proud.

Without ASTP, I probably would still be in rural Arkansas, where my folks were poor farmers.

Ed. Note: *Denton founded United Publishing Co. which spawned five trade magazines with offices in Atlanta and New York. In addition to his career in publishing and motivational lecturing, he founded exposition and convention management companies and served as chairman of Regions Bank of Atlanta until mandatory age retirement.*

Life Changers: ASTP and The GI Bill
by Joe B. Rushing (342nd Med Det)

ASTP: Last Chance to Enlist

After near blindness in my left eye blocked my enlistment in the Civilian Pilot Training program and all of the armed forces, I finally got in through the back door by applying for the ASTP program as a limited service enlistee. By the end of basic training both the ASTP program and the limited service loophole were closed down and I found my way via The Infantry Replacement Training Center at Camp Fannin and Camp Howze into the 86th Division where I served until my discharge in March 1946.

The GI Bill: Gateway to an unexpected and satisfying career

Upon my return from the Philippines in March, 1946, my career plans were set in concrete. I would return to college under the BI Bill, complete my bachelor's degree in chemistry and seek a job in industry. This plan held up until the end of the first summer term when I went to the office of the Dean to plan courses leading to graduation in January 1947. After reviewing my records, the dean announced, "Rushing, you have just graduated." Changes in degree requirements and correction of mistakes in my academic record led me into the graduation ceremony that very evening.

Before any prospective employer responded to my job resumes, the Dean told me that the Superintendent of Schools in Levelland, Texas, desperately needed a chemistry teacher. I agreed to take the job for a year after which I'd be free to go into industry. By mid year, however, I knew that I was just where I wanted to be. Thanks to the GI Bill, I returned to college for a teacher's certificate, then got a master's degree and, finally, after resigning my school principal's position I enrolled at the University of Texas, which two years later produced a PhD degree. And I still had left a few weeks of GI Bill eligibility!

In my opinion the GI Bill was one of the greatest pieces of legislation ever enacted.

A Tribute to the ASTP Whiz Kids
by Ernie Bavaria 342nd Sgt Major

At the 2006 reunion I took the mike to express how happy I was to be with my WWII comrades at a reunion made possible by the high quality people recognized as such by us "old timers" when you first joined up with us at Camp Livingston in '43. All of us who ever wore the Blackhawk patch have such a deep appreciation and gratitude to current officers and especially to those early officers who first established the Association with its first reunion in '84 and annual ones ever since.

If I didn't already have six years of active duty when I returned from the Philippines, I'm sure that'd have chosen the same path that most of you did. However, I liked the Army and remained on active duty and completed 24 years of service, which started with the 12th Infantry Band at Ft Howard, Maryland, and ended at the Aberdeen Proving Ground, Maryland, as adjutant of the Ordnance Center & School in late '63.

Upon receiving the '05 Membership Roster I immediately spotted the name of Capt. Arthur J. Dion—my boss in the 342nd. It was such a thrill to call him and make our first contact in sixty years. We had a long talk on the phone and looked forward to seeing each other at the '06 reunion in Falls Church, Virginia. Unfortunately it was not to be, and we were left to our memories of great times shared in the 86th Division.

FRANK CAMPANA....BLACKHAWK'S GIFT TO SHOW BIZ

Frank Campana with Tony Bennett

For those of us who've heard more than enough rap and hip hop leaking from our grandchildren's earphones, Frank Campana has the perfect antidote. It's a CD titled MEMORIES OF LOVE on which Frank croons a great selection of golden oldies, including "Old Black Magic," "As Time Goes By," "You'll Never Know" and "What is this thing Called Love?"

At Camp Livingston, Frank's day job was with the 86th Division MPs. He spent weekends in New Orleans as vocalist with the Blackhawk Big Band. After the war, he worked with the Dorsey brothers, who became lifelong friends, and got into a career of promoting artists whose names would fill an entertainers' encyclopedia, including Andy Griffith, Jim Nabors, Frankie Avalon, Tony Bennett (shown with Frank, above), Barbara Streisand and Johnny Cash. Currently Frank manages Johnny Cash's brother, Tommy Cash.

THE BLACKHAWK COMMANDOS
by Richard A. Phillips, 342nd B Co.

Possibly the least-known and never-used 86th troops were the Blackhawk Commandos, whose training for the Pacific Theater was overtaken by our assignment to Europe.

Rubber boat training was at the core of this specialized amphibious training. The idea was to prepare us to secretly paddle through the surf of an enemy-held island where we would check for underwater barbed wire or other obstacles, blow up a few things with plastic explosives and paddle back out unscathed. What a concept!

So, dressed in our uniforms of long johns and beanies, we practiced paddling out through the surf at Moro Bay and back in again. It would have been fun in the sun had it not been for the freezing water that turned our skin purple and kept our teeth chattering.

I don't recall the size of the unit, which consisted of individuals who could swim chosen from many companies. Each rubber boat was manned by a 10-member crew, and there were at least 30 boats. We thought of ourselves as a crack unit. We practiced close order drills, learned to use plastic explosives, and even acted in a training film on how to take a pillbox, complete with Bangalore torpedoes, flame throwers, grenades and all kinds of firepower.

The paddlers straddled each side of the boat. A cockswain in the rear steered with a paddle, and a sea anchor that looked like a wind sock was hung out the back to keep the boat straight coming in through the surf. If the boat came in at an angle, the surf would lift the boat up and dump its contents unceremoniously into the raging waves.

All went well until the final day of training. It was a night operation that scheduled a voyage down the bay, where we would go ashore to blow up a bridge or whatever before returning to our starting point. Our rifles and other weapons were strapped in the bottom of each boat, making them less seaworthy than before. The night was pitch black, and we soon learned that there was a storm brewing. The surf featured 20-foot breakers.

One man in each boat was given a flashlight to signal distress, and the boats went off into the darkness of the sea. Soon lights all over were signaling, boats were being flipped like toys. Some GIs were having water pumped out of them.

The decision was then made to scrap the operation and just paddle out through the surf. Well, only five boats out of 30 eventually made it. Our boat was one of the few to get out. As we paddled out through the breakers, the boat filled with water, but we kept going. Finally, it looked like a black wall in front of us. We feverishly paddled up to the top of it where we hung balanced while the wave broke under us. Down the other side, then up to and over the top of the next breaker, and finally we made it.

Coming back in, I was washed out of the boat and my leg got tangled in the rope of the sea anchor. I got loose, grabbed the side of the boat, and rode back in that way. Scary? You bet! It was one of the most frightening experiences I've ever had.

P.S. "Red" Goodrich, who was also selected for this amphibious training, managed to use an injury caused by a flying paddle released by the comrade sitting in front of him to get out of that horrendous night exercise. The scalp wound was only the size of a quarter but required an impressive gauze bandage to be wrapped over and around his head. Red used this apparently disabling injury to stay bedridden in his San Luis Obispo hut for several days. Until one night the ragged bandage fell off to reveal—nothing.

21st Reunion Memorial Address
by Dr. Robert M. Bookbinder 343 1st Bn Hq Co

Former Association President, Bob Bookbinder

I am deeply honored and privileged this morning to stand before you as we memorialize and do honor to those 86th Blackhawk Division comrades whose names have just been read, those comrades who gave their last full measure of devotion in Germany or the Philippines and all Blackhawks who have gone to their eternal rest since World War II some sixty years ago. This memorial message was to have been delivered by our recently deceased bother and comrade in arms, the Reverend Richard Mapes, of blessed memory, and I shall, to the best of my ability, attempt to fill his very large shoes.

Now the hour of reunion has arrived
In this room devoid of mirth and cheer;

And silence descends as if from heaven,
Upon the group assembled here.

Slowly die the fire's last embers,
As this moment grows still and serene,

And we honor our absent comrades,
Who have passed beyond the scene;

We behold with eyes grown older,
With eyes that have a magic scope,

Life's abandoned fires that smolder
On the distant trail of hope

And our memories are beguiling
When the lights are soft and low,

For we see our comrades smiling
As they smiled long years ago.

So to you our absent comrades
With our hearts and hands held high,

We lower our eyes and honor your sweet memories
That will never, never die.

    This memorial service is always deeply moving, because it brings before our minds a flow of memories, and the faces of those very young comrades who wore the Blackhawk shoulder patch, as we did, those many years ago. They were, we were, members of that infantry division that was often warmly referred to as "The Kids Division."

    Today, we look into the mirror of the past and we remember those members of the 86th who were killed in action, as well as those comrades in arms who have also gone to their eternal rest since that period of WW II. In our memories, their voices ring out again and again. Their faces remind us of all that was and is no more. We are caught up in two emotions. We are deeply saddened for the losses we have suffered, and yet we are comforted in the knowledge that these friends, these comrades in arms, have left their mark upon our world, for they had helped save it from enslavement. They left their mark upon their families, for they had brought them life, and laughter and strength. They had left their mark upon all of us, they had become closer to us than brothers.

All the promises that life held out to them were buried with them, and all the Crosses and Stars of David appear as a sea of waving hands, reaching upwards in a gesture of farewell.

The historian William Manchester was known to say, "I can never forget all that happened to me. Therefore, wherever I go there are always two persons present. One is an eighteen-year-old wearing a steel helmet and fatigues with a quick step and a sharp tongue. The other is gray-haired and has trouble with the print in the telephone books. But they are both there, wherever I go, whatever I do."

We are gathered here today, to pay honor to their memories and to show, in a very real way, the high regard in which they are kept by us all. We are all saddened beyond belief. The feelings that continue to pass among us, feelings that their deaths have left us, the remaining members of the 86th Blackhawk Infantry Division, and their families, with a void that can never be entirely filled. All of us present sense this to our abiding sorrow. Our only consolation is the knowledge that we were privileged to know and serve side-by-side in the military with them during WW II and continued our warm and friendly relationships with the many who survived, but passed on during these past 60 years.

There are some things in this world that, try as we may, just cannot be adequately done. One of these things is to express adequately what we feel about the passing of our fellow comrades in arms. We are the slaves of words. All too often, they are all we have to express those wordless feelings that so fill our minds and hearts. Yes, words are all we have, and yet at times such as these, they simply are not enough. We use a word like sorrow, but what does it convey? We are faced at this moment where each of us, in his and her heart is reminded of an intense personal loss. Each of us feel it, carry it and live with it, because someone we cherished so very much has been removed from our lives. And yet, all we have is a word like sorrow.

We try to describe what we feel for our friends and fellow comrades in arms and again we are stuck with words. We use a word like honor, but what does that really mean? Why, we all stand as living proof of the greatness, bravery and self-sacrifice of our comrades. We saw and know of their dedication; we were witness to their care and concern; we stood in awe of their great camaraderie, we whispered prayers of thanks that we were privileged to be associated with persons of their worth.

And to sum up what they were and what they did, we use a word like love. We saw our friends and comrades pour forth love as they trained, drilled, marched, crawled and fought by our sides. We saw their warmth and compassion. We were privy to the hours and hours of exhausting toil and training they put into perfecting their military skills in order that they might be the best they could be. Our hearts swell with the memories of how they lived that word—that word love.

Yet we are heartened by the fact that rather than words, we will use our memories, those images that are inscribed within our hearts, to keep them alive within us—that legacy of love and honor which was their lives and which, in truth can never die. For they were with us during basic training, during those early reveillies, at the rifle range, during bayonet drill, on the short forced marches, the all nighters, the obstacle courses and manuevers at Howze and Livingston. They were with us as we continued our training, paraded and attacked the hills at San Luis Obispo. They were also with us as we ran ashore from those assault boats to capture and recapture that famed island called San Clemente at Callan.

And they were with us as we made our way across the country and boarded ships crossing the rough seas of the North Atlantic to Le Havre, France. Dthey were with us as we literally froze in those bitterly cold tents at Camp Old Gold during March of 1945. And they were with us as we made our way with the 22nd Corps of the 15th Army through Aachen and Duren to our very first battle site at Ossendorf, Cologne, Germany. They may have been among those brave fellows in those assault boats who scouted the eastern shore of the Rhein, within sight of the great cathedral at Cologne, Germany, and capture our first German prisoners.

And then they were with us as we made our way south, crossed the Rhein between between Bonn and Remagen and on April 4th 1945, made our way into the Ruhr with the 18th Airborne Corps of the 1st Army. They were also with us when the 86th captured Banfe, Hilchenbach, Benolp, Repe, Attendorn, Rebbin, Herscheid, Augustenthal, Ossenburg, Altena,

Hagen, and Siegen. And during these battles in the Ruhr, some died, others were wounded, and still others learned, however briefly, what it meant to become a POW.

And they were with us as we joined the 3rd Army on April 19th to battle in Krasspheim, Wurzburg, Nurnburg and Ansbach. Those who remained with us, on April 21, 1945, fought with the 15th Corps of the7th Army as we made our way further into Bavaria and into Austria through Kulbingen, St. Veit, Eichstaff, Sappefeld, Ingolstadt (on the Danube) Waal, Kirchdorf, Freising, Eerding, Ellingen, Buch, Pischelsdorf and Gilgenberg. They crossed the Altmul, Danube and Isar rivers into the Bavarian Redoubt, where we liberated Russian and Polish slave laborers and captured many German soldiers, including members of the hated SS.

Let us now pay a very special tribute to the founders of our 86th Blackhawk Division Association who have gone to their eternal rest: Jim "Whitey" Woznick, Sam Setzer, Dale Durant, Russ Wincentsen, kFrank Smith, George Rau, John Schuepach, Gene Puhl, Bug Hogate, Gottleib Schock, Harry Nicholson and "Pop" Tilton. We are here today art this reunion, because they had a vision and a mission. There were among the leaders who saw to the creation of the 86th Division Association.

On April 19, 1945, Maj. General Harris Melasky, the commanding officer of the 86th Division wrote: "Words of praise are hardly sufficient to convey the high regard and confidence I have in the Blackhawk Division and the fighting traditions it forged for itself in the annihilation of German fortresses in the "Battle of the Ruhr Pocket.... Later Gen. Melasky added: "I can think of no more fitting tribute to the valiant deeds of the men of this Division than to say that you accomplished what I expected and had faith you would do.... I am indeed honored to have commanded the Blackhawk Division." As we near the closing moments of this annual reunion ... we once more think of them, we see their faces, we hear their voices, the bond that binds us is still there. It is a bond forged in suffering, peril and death. But above all it is a bond of selflessness, sharing, and great heartedness—and always humor, wit and laughter. We feel that here, today for we know that they live within us, and we also know their spirits continue to glow with the brilliance they manifested while they were among us. As they honored us with their lives, we now honor them within our hearts and minds. They had simply done what had to be done. And for this we have gathered here to honor them, because of all they were—whether they had walked on this green earth for only 19 years or eighty. As we near the closing moments of this annual reunion of the 86th Blackhawk Division Association, we once more think of them, we see their faces, we hear their voices, the bond that binds us is still there. It is a bond forged in suffering, peril and death. But, above all, it is a bond of selflessness, sharing, and great heartedness—and always humor, wit and laughter.

As long as we live, they too will live, for they are now, as they were in those earlier years, a part of us, as we remember them. **Amen.**

Note: *Dr. Robert "Bob" Bookbinder served as President of the 86th Blackhawk Division Association for four years (2000—2004); edited the Blackhawk Bugle newsletter during most of this period and managed the Association PX. He also got published three books about the 86th Division and organized the "Harmonicats," musical combo which performed at four annual reunions.*

PART TWO

EUROPEAN THEATER

The Prologue: Departed Boston Port February 19, 1945
Arrived Le Havre, France, March 3
Departed Le Havre area, March 24

The Battles: The Rhine, March 6 to April 4
The Ruhr, April 7 to April 16
Bavaria, April 22 to May 8

The Victory: German Prisoners Taken: 53,354
German Territory Covered 220 Miles
Rivers Forced: Bigge, Altmuhl, Danube, Isar, Isar Mittel, Inn, Salzach

The Epilogue: Departed Germany, May 30, 1945
Departed Le Havre, June 7, 1945
Arrived New York, June 17,1945

A Breathless Passage
by Chuck Bernstein, 343rd L Co.

At dawn, 19 Feb 1945, shouldering heavy barracks bags, the 86th Blackhawk Division jostles its determined way amid the deafening bustle and hubbub of busy Boston Harbor to reach their ocean liner converted to a U.S. Army Transport ship. The curtain of thick gray mist only partly mutes the deafening thunder of loading and unloading.

We're part of a convoy of perhaps fifty ships of all shapes and sizes, from cargo carriers to robust oil and chemical tankers. There is a comforting addition of a few deadly, defiant-looking Cruisers, Destroyers and even an Aircraft Carrier cum Heliport, plus a pair of tiny siren-screaming Corvettes sent by Canada, added assurance that the U.S. Navy would get us safely to Europe. Helicopters clatter noisily, circling overhead.

A placid week or so after our startling first middle of the night, on-deck practice "Lifeboat Drill," and now, after an uneventful voyage and perhaps only three days out from Le Havre, our final destination, the ship's bells clanging loudly in the bitterly cold night wakes us. We are called to what we think is just another dry run Lifeboat Drill.

But this time, via the ship's radio, stentorian orders: BATTLE STATIONS, BATTLE STATIONS! NAVAL PERSONNEL, MAN YOUR POSTS!

Then: "THIS IS *NOT* A DRILL! REPEAT: THIS IS *NOT* A DRILL!"

This confirms our ground-bound Infantryman's worst fears. I don't know about the others, but before my heart returns to steadily anging away in my chest, it had skipped several uncountable beats.

Then: "THIS IS THE CAPTAIN SPEAKING. ARMY PERSONNEL STAY BELOW! PUT ON YOUR LIFE BELT OR LIFE JACKET AND STAND BY YOUR ASSIGNED BUNK READY TO COME ON DECK ON COMMAND! DO NOT CLOG THE GANGWAYS OR THE SHIP'S LADDERS."

In my mind's eye I see us being dunked into the dark frigid seawater far from shore with little chance of imminent rescue, inasmuch as over time the ships in our convey have moved *miles apart*, and are far out of sight!

I'm nervous enough, when some guy in obvious despair whispers to me, "Sarge, I can't even swim!" Trying to look cool, I smile and say, "Neither can I! But with our life belts we can float together like two ducks." That gets the kid to laugh and I seriously think, *We'll have perhaps three minutes of life in these waters, swim or float.*

Peripherally and of incidental interest at the moment are the on-their-knees poker players and crap-shooters who let us all know that they are extremely *unhappy* at being interrupted mid-game "by the damned Germans!" Stern warnings are heard that "if so much as a quarter disappears from this pot, there'll be hell to pay."

In mainly breathless silence we all wait, hold our breath, and wait … and wait … and it seems like forever, while the ship veers sharply then seems to circle. Finally the silence is broken by the sound (or maybe more the *feel*) of three dull-sounding underwater explosions, or more accurately, *concussions* far below us!

Seconds later, still wary, we all inhale and wait, while again, the guys whisper hopeful guesses, "*Depth bombs?* Were those *depth bombs?*"

The answer to the guessing is confirmed by simultaneous trembling reverberations (or are they echoes?) and then the noticeable shuddering of our ship's hull. We can only stand by our assigned bunks, and hope we, the *Good Guys*, "got" the enemy menace and knocked out what was actually a German U-boat that, we are later surprisingly told, "has been stalking us *since we left Boston.*"

Some thought it must be the Canadian Corvettes that did the sub in. Later we learn that we owe thanks to our own ship's perceptive *sonar experts and Navy crewmen* for literally saving our lives. (*And incidentally saving several craps and poker games and their players from oblivion.*)

At last, we hear the clangor of the ship's bell and the Captain's calm, bass voice over the intercom: "ALL CLEAR! ALL CLEAR! IN THIRTY MINUTES, ARMY PERSONNEL ARE FREE TO COME ON DECK. KNOW THAT THE SUB WE SANK MAY'VE BEEN PART OF A 'PACK.' THEY USUALLY RUN IN PACKS. REMEMBER THAT WE ARE STILL IN 'STRICT BLACKOUT CONDITIONS. NO SMOKING AND NO LIGHTS TOPSIDE!"

We're relieved. Free to breathe normally and talk again! I clamber up on deck as fast as I can to inhale a deep breath of fresh, clean ocean air.

And as I'm about to leave the hold, I find the gamblers are already back down on their knees. As if nothing had happened, they are busily, noisily, and happily back in business.

On deck I race aft to search out between the waves and the ship's bubbling, gurgling white wake if I can perceive any piece of the sunken submarine, the hateful and scary German U-Boat. It's dark, windy and bitter cold. The sea is as blacked out as is our ship. And I silently thank God and our ship's personnel that I'm not floundering around, freezing in the water, waiting for rescue.

Editor: This story is reprinted from "Chuck" Bernstein's book: BLACKHAWK MISSION: In Europe and the Pacific in WW II. Available via www. iUniverse.com or telephone: 1–800–288–4677 ext.501.

Memoirs of a Bazooka Man
by Bob Rasmus, 342nd L Co.

Watching a number of WWII documentaries on TV at the time of the 60th anniversary of VE-Day, as an ex-bazooka man I paid particular attention whenever bazooka action was shown. Naturally I thought a lot about my own bazooka experiences, and it hit me for the first time—one way or another they were all embarrassments.

The first occurred at Camp San Luis Obispo during a mock attack against a simulated Japanese pillbox. It called for a whole range of weapons—small arms, Bangalore torpedoes, a bazooka—to blast a hole in the pillbox, and a flame-thrower to shoot liquid fire into it. As the bazooka man, I was called up to do the blasting. I pulled the trigger and—deadly silence! Unbeknownst to me the batteries needed to fire the rocket had fallen out of their compartment. What a humiliation! A beautiful exercise screwed up by one man: me.

Fortunately, when we arrived in Europe, we were issued new bazookas that used magnetos instead of batteries. The first chance I had for a practice shot was just outside Breidenbach, the town where the next day we would begin our Ruhr Pocket campaign. I found a good target—the entrance to a cave at the bottom of a hill. I fired, missed the cave completely, as the rocket hit halfway up the hill. Fortunately, only a few witnessed this second embarrassment.

Three days later, we were moving through a forest shrouded in early morning fog. The company was stretched out in a single column with my platoon in the lead. Suddenly we were stopped in our tracks. The lead scouts had spotted a German tank ahead. I heard the dreaded words: "send Rasmus up." Gulp! As my ammo bearer and I moved up the line, passing buddies along the way, several couldn't resist wisecracking, "Hey, Ras, yuh got your batteries?"

I reached the scouts at the edge of a clearing. The fog had thinned enough for me to see the tank 60 or 70 yards away, looking every bit as menacing as I feared it would. My first round was a direct hit, just below the main gun! Ditto, the second, and I turned my head back to tell my ammo man we'd go for a third. Then I turned around to see Lt. Norman, our company exec, standing atop the tank, his carbine pointed through the opened hatch. Norman was a swashbuckling, fearless officer, a cowboy from Oklahoma, and I shouldn't have been surprised. He had sensed the tank was out of fuel and abandoned, and had climbed up to confirm his hunch. So much for my "moment of glory."

That was the end of my bazooka career. We soon realized that the Wehrmacht's "panzerfaust" (mailed fist) was more effective than our bazooka and these could be picked up where German troops had abandoned them. These were used a few times to blast holes in concrete walls in urban fighting. And I was glad to return to being a regular rifleman.

As I reflect on all this 60 years later, I realize that in spite of my chagrin at the time, I did retain a sense of pride that I had been cool enough to hit the tank—twice! I was scared, but I hadn't seen enough combat at that point to be really scared. That changed by the end of that day, but that's another story. (**Editor's note:** Stay tuned.)

The Day The War Got Real
by Bob Rasmus, 342nd L Co.

Bob Rasmus

April 10, 1945, was the day the war got real and I grew up. Until that day, WWII as I experienced it was exciting, even dramatic, but I felt no genuine pain. I was nineteen, unmarried, and something of a romantic. I read Thomas Wolfe's "Look Homeward, Angel!" on the troopship coming over and each episode up to that day virtually had the quality of a newsreel.

The excitement began way back in Boston Harbor in February when, from the deck of our troop transport (the converted Swedish-America liner *Kungsholm*) I viewed an Australian battle cruiser tied up at the adjoining dock with a huge jagged hole in its bow. It was my first look at an actual battle casualty. Wow, real action!

Crossing the Atlantic in the great convoy was an even more dramatic experience, and this was heightened as I watched destroyer escorts launching depth charges to sink prowling German subs. Moving across northern France and Belgium to Germany in the legendary *40 & 8's* to the acclaim of cheering civilians was another exciting episode. Our first exposure to enemy fire was mostly sporadic exchanges with Germans across the Rhine given a special aura of excitement by the movie "Watch on the Rhine."

I started to wonder whether the Germans were collapsing so fast that we were actually going to be lucky enough to get through the rest of the war without casualties. If so, it would be the best of all possible worlds. We would have experienced the excitement and drama of war without suffering any losses. But as that day of April 10th wore on, the script changed. The sporadic firing off in the distance began to intensify and moved closer. A sense of foreboding crept in, and even the terrain got tougher. As we plodded through the forests the trees seemed to become more tangled and the hills got steeper. Finally we stopped for a break near the top of a hill. Almost immediately our acting platoon leader, Tech. Sgt. Earl Roat, told us in a low voice that there were German troops just down the hill. Staying low, we were to form a single line and when Captain McSpadden started firing we were to get up and attack with marching fire. Just like that! The opening shot from McSpadden came, we began marching fire, and the Germans returned fire surprisingly fast.

Firing in both directions was intense, rose in a crescendo, and then suddenly stopped. With the advantage of surprise, we killed at least half the Germans—we later counted 20 dead. The rest took off through the woods. As soon as the firing stopped I was horrified to see the bodies of Roat and Pfc Robert Johns lying on the ground, both dead. Their faces were waxen. A bullet had gone through Roat's neck, and blood was seeping out onto the ground. A segment of Johns' skull was gone—blown away. My God! It had happened so quickly, was so final, so irreversible!

That was the moment of transformation, the moment when the war became horrible and real. It was no longer a series of exciting episodes. It was now a grim confrontation with death.

As a lowly Pfc, a bottom link in the chain of command, I visualized the situation only getting worse. I saw our platoon radioman throw down his heavy radio and shoot holes in it, presumably to make it useless to the enemy, and it made me wonder if we were going to retreat. We received orders from McSpadden to move out and he soberly added, "pick up the bodies, we don't leave our dead to the enemy." So we actually *were* retreating? (Only later did I learn that we were simply "repositioning" ourselves relative to other companies in the battalion.)

Eventually we stretcher-bearers couldn't keep up with the company and had to leave the bodies behind. Finally we reached a place in the forest where we would spend the night. As darkness descended we dug slit trenches, guards were assigned, and we tried to get some sleep. Since I was without a field jacket, I tried to stay warm by covering myself with pine boughs. I slept fitfully and experienced a series of nightmares. The impact of the two deaths was apparently so great that each of my squad buddies appeared in the nightmare, one by one—dead. Each of their faces had the same waxen look of Roat and Johns. in the night, without any preliminaries, an 88 shell hit in the trees. It exploded with a tremendous blast, spraying shrapnel in all directions. There was a second or two of silence and then came the cries of "medic," medic, over here!" Pfc Ray Helinsky had been killed, and five of our people were wounded, four seriously. One a company medic, Dean Naden, was paralyzed from the waist down. More shock and sorrow. The rest of the night was spent listlessly, some still trying to sleep, others simply waiting, thinking. Many must have been going through the same mental calculation I was—one that all infantrymen make: "*It's just a matter of time.*" On that day we had had three killed and five wounded. How many days like that does it take to go through a company of fewer than two hundred?

From that point on every day for me was dominated by the thought of death or serious wounding. In hindsight we know that as of April 10 the war in Europe had less than a month to go, so we were spared from that grim arithmetic playing out. But we didn't know it at the time. Even General Bradley was uncertain, and as late as April 24th he told a group of visiting congressmen that because of the possibility of a National Redoubt for German forces in Bavaria and Austria the war could go on for another year.

And even though the war in the European Theater ended on May 8, we had to realistically expect to be sent to the Pacific to fight the Japanese. In fact this grim prospect appeared to be reality shortly after VE Day when we returned home en route to the Pacific. So the grim arithmetic of "*it's just a matter of time*" remained with us until the A-bombs were dropped in August.

Captain Mac and Me
by Austin "Red" Goodrich, 342nd K Co.

Captain "Mac"

My first encounter with Capt. Bruce Macalister, Commanding Officer of Company K, 342nd Infantry Regiment of the 86th Division, was an unhappy experience. We were on field maneuvers in the backwoods of central Louisiana and I had left my Colt .45 automatic slung from my pistol belt hanging on a tree branch before a sudden rain shower drove us into the dubious shelter of our pup tents. It may have been the debilitating heat that caused me to forget my sidearm. (Marching in the midday sun even for an hour or two had caused so many troops to suffer heat exhaustion that long marches were usually scheduled after sundown.) Or it may have been that my need to catch some shut-eye overrode my duty to first clean my pistol and put it in a secure place.

I might have subconsciously thought that as a light machine gunner my duty extended only to the care and feeding of my Browning Model 1917 machine gun. (Had I not spent countless late night hours in the latrine cleaning *that* sonuvabitch after a few thousand rounds of filthy .30 caliber blanks had charred its innards?) But that was no excuse. There was in fact no excuse for leaving a pistol belt hanging on a tree limb in the rain. I was summoned to appear before Capt. MacAlister in his command tent.

"Do you know where your pistol is, Goodrich?"

"No, sir."

"Could this be it?"

"Yes sir, it looks like it," I responded lamely as a knot began to build in my throat.

"Your sidearm was found hanging from the branch of a tree. Now how in the world do you suppose it got there?"

"I must have put it there, sir."

"Well I'd say that's a dumb place to put a pistol, wouldn't you?"

"Yes sir." Standing at attention, fear filled with humiliation turned my knees into gelatin and I could feel the shakes moving from my shoulders to my feet. Captain Mac, clearly aware of this 18-year-old's discomfort brought the inquiry to a conclusion. His piercingly blue eyes looked up at me as he passed sentence. "I want you to clean this pistol until it looks like new," he said calmly as he handed it to me. Then he reached behind him with his other hand to retrieve the pistol belt and its empty holster, which he gave me, saying: "When you've finished cleaning it, bring your .45 to Lt. Morris (company exec, a former bank guard known to have little use for the college boys serving at the bottom of K company ranks). He'll inspect it."

"Yes, sir" rasped its way up through my tinder dry throat. I turned to leave but stopped, turned around and saluted. "I'm sorry."

"S' okay, said my CO under his breath. I thought I caught a glimpse of a smile as he looked up to return my salute.

* * * * * *

After more than a year of training for the Pacific Theatre—jungle training in Louisiana and amphibious training in southern California, we unexpectedly found ourselves at Camp Lucky Strike, a staging area in northern France. Even for a boy who grew up in Michigan, the damp, blustery cold of Normandy in January, 1945, was hard to take. Fortunately I had a heavy-duty olive drab wool scarf knit by my mom. She had started it when I was assigned to Camp Blanding, Florida, and continued the needlework through my stays in a series of warm-weather posts. Despairing of my ever getting into cold weather, she just kept on knitting until she finally sent the six-foot long scarf to me in sunny California, where it provided a good laugh for my hut mates. A few months later the last laugh was mine. While my shaved-head comrades shivered, I coiled the long scarf over my head, around my throat and across my chest against the sub-zero winds whistling off the North Sea. Nevertheless, I came down with a terrible head cold, but that didn't keep me from a football game against our arch rivals in "I" Company. Played on frozen tundra, the game which was to be "two-hands touch" quickly turned into smash-mouth tackle without benefit of helmets or pads of any kind. Captain Mac was a one-man cheering section on the sideline. Out of the corner of my eye, I saw him shout and pump his arm when I took down an opponent with a vicious cross-body block to clear the way for our punt return man to score.

That evening I paid the price. My throat was so swollen I could barely speak, and I went to the mess tent with my canteen cup to get a teaspoon of salt and some hot water to gargle. Captain Mac was there with a mug of coffee.

"You really love to play football don't you, Goodrich?"

"Yesssir," I squeaked, "I guess I do." There flashed through my subconscious a montage of happy times playing on vacant lots as a kid, as a 180 lb. guard/tackle in high school (All State honorable mention) and scrimmaging with Elroy "Crazy Legs" Hirsch and other V-12 All Americans on the Univ. of Michigan practice field in the late summer of '43.

"You know, you shouldn't play football when you have such a bad cold," said this man who obviously loved the game as much as I did. This showed in the warmth of a smile that spread across his Scottish grenadier's face made redder than usual by the cold and possibly a dram or two of the local home-brewed 120-proof Calvados apple brandy.

"I guess not." I returned his smile as my love for this man warmed me all over.

* * * * * *

The balls-out offensive led by Gen. Patton that swept us forward after our baptism of fire in the Ruhr pocket suited Captain Mac just fine. He was born to lead, not only in the sense of providing direction, but physically as well. Always in the vanguard, he loved the tactic of *marching fire*, which dictated that infantry units encountering enemy fire would advance while firing their weapons in the direction of the enemy instead of looking for cover or digging foxholes. This took real leadership. You knew you were the specific target for death when the sharp crack of a single rifle shot, or the fabric-ripping tear of a Schmeitzer machine pistol rent the air above your noggin. The natural reaction was to duck down and look for a place to hide. To do otherwise was and is an unnatural act requiring what some would call courage, and others would call lunacy. In these situations, our CO was always the first one up, firing his carbine and shouting to those within earshot to get up, get going, start shooting. I learned to fire my machine gun from the hip while moving forward to provide maximum firepower.

Unfortunately, I was providing covering fire for troops to cross a stretch of open field on the edge of the town of Berglern in Bavaria when Captain Mac went down. When I reached a barn on the edge of a field where he lay wounded, our brave medic was calling for automatic weapons fire to cover him so he could reach our wounded CO.

And I was out of ammunition.

Members of "I" Company were moving up from reserve and I saw a light machine gun squad with several boxes of ammunition. I wanted to ask if I could borrow one of the olive drab canisters, but I froze, and I don't know why. I guess I never heard of anybody asking to borrow ammunition. Maybe I was embarrassed to ask. Maybe I was afraid to.

That night we learned that our medic had reached our beloved captain who had a gut shot and needed more than first aid. The only hope was to get him to a field hospital. There were no evac helicopters and our high-speed advance had put three waterways—the Danube, Isar rivers and the Isar Mittel canal—between us and the nearest aid station. One could say that Captain Mac's determination to end the war as soon as possible, or sooner, cost him his life. But to this day I blame myself for lacking the guts to ask for—or simply grab—a box of ammo.

I'm left with bittersweet feelings of love and guilt, silent prayers for my fallen captain whispered at Veterans of Foreign Wars meetings and an ingrained determination to deal with adversity by standing up and marching straight ahead.

A Slice of Combat ... and Baloney
by Charles H. "Bernie" Bernstein 343rd L Co.

One of my squad's scariest moments in the whole war was the night I stood astride a cliff at the front of a Sherman tank, its 75mm gun in its mobile turret moving from side to side while its machine-gunner spurted a steady stream of fiery red tracer bullets just inches over my head and my CO ordering me to jump off the cliff into total darkness with my squad following.

I was bothered by the proximity of the stream of tracers streaking so close over my helmet and concerned if the machine gunner lowered the muzzle of his gun in the slightest he could wipe out my squad, me included. I was also concerned that in the darkness, I had no idea how far from the top of the cliff I would fall before landing. And landing on what? Nevertheless, signaling my squad to follow, I blindly jumped, and my "lemmings" obediently jumped after me....

Once the squad got moving, dodging the zinging of the enemy's bullets, our concerns about jumping down into the dark unknown rapidly turned to gratitude for the presence of the American Sherman tank and its sure-fingered gunners. Together we decimated and finally extirpated the reputably "invincible" soldiers of the world's "Master Race" just as the sun started to rise in the east.

I've heard it said that once a soldier is shot at a few times he becomes used to it. Does anyone become used to being shot at? You can get used to wearing tennis shoes or eating corn flakes for breakfast, but I do not buy the idea that a live target at rifle practice becomes so inured to being shot at that he doesn't consider it more than a triviality. Baloney!

TEXAS BAR-B-Q: Austrian Style
by Bill Severin 343rd I Co*

Every company had its zany characters who were usually very happy people. Happy people go around repelling unhappiness like evil—not wanting to be tainted by anyone's bad luck. Our happy man was a Texan named Norman Stewart, who came to us from a replacement training center and immediately became a BAR man in the second platoon. From our earliest days in Europe, Norman proved to be a forager without equal. He was always on the prowl, frisking along doing his best to repel low spirits. He was one to avoid problems, whiners, complaints, envious questions and urgencies of any kind.

Norman came into his own when we entered Cologne. This was his kind of place. While others were content to just follow routine he was out "looking around" by day and, especially, by night. He was the one to come up with Grundig radios, rare wines, flags, pieces of German uniforms and jewelry. However, his great coup was a suitcase full of German money. Norman always claimed he was going through the woods and found it near a staff car, but no one could ever recall him mentioning anything about it until we heard about one of the banks in a bypassed village having its vault blown late one night.

Norman carried his suitcase with him from just past Ingolstadt until we reached Austria. Everyone kept telling him that German money was no good and he was foolish to keep lugging it around, until we settled into our little compound east of Pischeldorf, Austria. The war was over and a celebration was in order. Norman knew how to deal with the farmer where our platoon was billited. He bought a cow with most of the German money. Actually, he forced packets of his cash on the poor peasant. Norman figured it had no value, so let's live it up!

Fast forward to our Camp Kilmer. One of our sergeants took his money to see if he could change it into U.S. Dollars. Lo and behold, he got $800 U.S.. Word spread like wildfire. The money was good! Norman almost fainted.

Some 45 yeas later, my wife and I returned to Pischeldorf to see the farmhouse, but it was gone. In its place was an imposing chalet that stuck out like the Sears Tower in Chicago! Was it possible that poor peasant turned into a rich farmer overnight? No one knows what became of Norman, but we are sure that his memories of the captured German money will always be with him.

Saving Our Own "Pvt. Ryan"
by Bill Severin, 343rd I Co

Remembering people from our days in the war reminded me that people's principal possessions were their stories. Though I never wrote them down, the young men's faces clothes, names and accounts have stayed with me and are easily recalled.

The fact is, we had our own Pvt. Ryan in I Co. His real name was Leo Zitsch, and he was a skinny kid from the rough side of Elizabeth, NJ. He was articulate, open-minded, hospitable, charismatic, and highly intelligent.

Leo told us about his two brothers who were also in the army. Since Leo was the youngest, they were always writing him with good advice on how to manage his life during this stressful time. Both siblings were in the infantry, one in the 1st Division and the other in the 26th Division.

The news of his oldest brother being killed in Normandy came on a July day in Camp Livingston. Leo was granted an emergency furlough so he could go home and grieve with his family. However, life goes on. The next blow fell just before we were getting ready to leave for San Luis Obispo, CA and our trip to Europe. His second brother was killed in action during heavy fighting in the Huertgen Forest. Again Leo went home to grieve with his stunned family. When he returned from New Jersey Leo was told to see the Chaplain, who told him he was going to be reassigned to a non-combat unit and would stay in the States. Guess what? Leo said he'd rather stay with I Company. Our Sergeant Platt, a very wise old man (age 25) talked to Leo and tried to get him to see that reassignment would be a wise move, but no luck. Leo wanted to stay with his buddies.

I last talked with Leo Zitsch in September 1947 when we had a reunion at Sgt. Platt's farm in upstate New York. I wanted to ask him why he stayed but I never did. All these years that question has remained in my brain. Now I know I will never get an answer as Leo Zitsch has died, and the answer has died with him.

Recollection of a Gravel-Clutcher*
by Austin Goodrich 342nd K Co.

"Red" Goodrich

So you have pain now; but I will see you again, and your hearts will rejoice, and no one will take your joy from you. John 16:22

I don't think much about the World War II now, even though this year marks the passage of over 50 years since it ended. I'm just comforted to know I had some wee small part in its outcome.

Sometimes events of the past are either reduced to insignificance by people born after them, or enlarged beyond recognition by nostalgic reminiscences. Still, every once in a while, I can hear again that cry in the woods high on a ridge overlooking the town of Hilchenbach in the Ruhr Valley ...

Our unit had marched all day and was looking forward to some rest when the order came down: we would soon take part in our first large-scale night attack. We were to wait in the woods above the village while our artillery and air support dropped high explosives on the targeted town. Then we were to attack and take over the town.

Toward evening, we took our places. At first, the whining sound of shells passing overhead was largely ignored. But gradually the shells came closer to the tops of the pine trees where we waited, until there was only a split second between the whining sound and the explosion.

Then there was no interval at all, and we were under the worst kind of friendly fire: huge shell bursts that spewed down jagged shreds of steel in sweeping arcs of destruction. Nobody was standing or sitting now: it was time to dig a hole in the ground and hide. At the base of a large tree, I pawed at the ground, sending pine needles flying. The explosions overhead got so intense that individual bursts merged into an ear-splitting roll of deadly thunder. And I prayed: *Oh, God, please, please make 'em stop. Please God ...*

Then, very suddenly, there was a terrible silence. It was over, but no one spoke, and bodies rose up like ghosts from a graveyard. Finally, calls were heard from different parts of the hillside: *Medic, over here! Hurry! Help, Medic!*

It was then that I heard, through the scattered calls for help, the one cry that has remained with me all these years. The voice was that of PFC Marks, a rifleman in the 3rd Platoon. Like many of us in the 86th, Walter Marks had been slated to go to college when the war interrupted. I remember him as a smiling person with the impish look of a boy always on the verge of pulling off a great practical joke.

His voice traveled through the woods with a special resonance that overrode the cries for help and sounds of battle.

One word, spoken once. "Mother!"

Curious, I thought. The voice lacked the unmistakable sound of pain, nor did it hold any hint of desperation or even sorrow. It was more like a greeting.

When we were finally marching down to take the town, I chanced to see our company medic.

"Did you see Marks back there"

"Yeah."

"Wounded?"

"No, killed."

"But I heard him call out."

"So did I, but I don't know how."

And on we went to do our duty.

If I had known Marks better, I thought, *I would try to find his mother when this was over and tell her she was the last thing in her son's heart when he died.* But I hadn't even known his first name, and as often happened, I was unable to continue to deal with death consciously—I blocked out the details in all my worst nightmares.

Some of our old Company K buddies recently got together to celebrate the golden anniversary of our survival. One of them had been a close friend of Marks'. I asked him about our fallen friend's last moments, and if he'd heard that call. He had.

"He must have seen his mother in his mind's eye and called out to her," I suggested.

"You know, I've often wondered about that," the friend replied, "because Walter never knew his mother. He had never even seen her."

"How's that?"

"She died in childbirth when she brought him into this world."

* This story was first published in *CHICKEN SOUP FOR THE CHRISTIAN SOUL*

HOW WAYNE MICKIE MARTIN FOUGHT THE WAR!
by Wayne Mickie Martin 341st G Co.

"Mickey," West Virginia Rifleman

Service wise, I passed the Aviation Cadet exam and while working at a seaplane base, I learned to solo a seaplane. I then found out I was eligible for a third alternate appointment to West Point. I thought I would take six months of free college, then switch over to Aviation Cadets. After six months of West Point prep, the Belgian Bugle sent me to Camp

Livingston to join a bunch of washed-out cadets and ASTPers. I had no basic training at all and had never even seen an M-1 rifle up close.

I was dumped into the 1st Platoon, G. Co. 341st Inf., 86th Division, where I learned how to assemble my field pack and how not to get my leggings tangled by lacing them up on the insides. There was a fire and maneuver exercise with live ammunition planned. The next day we proceeded to this hill, disembarked and were each issued a clip of live ammunition. I was ashamed to admit that I did not know how to load an M-1 rifle. I pulled the bolt back and that part looked full to me. I figured, maybe, that they are supposed to go in from the bottom. I pulled on the trigger-guard and ended up with the trigger housing in my right hand, the barrel in my left hand and the stock on the ground. The Sergeant said "What the hell are you doing, Red?" I said, "How do you put the bullets in this gun, Sarge?" He grabbed my ammo clip and said, "Mueller, put this man's rifle back together." I said, "What do I do when it's my turn to shoot?" He said, "You simulate", I said, "What do you mean 'simulate'?" He said, "When we fire and maneuver up the hill, and it comes your turn to shoot, you yell BANG real loud." I thought, "Man, if this is what the army is, I want to go home". I finally adjusted, to a degree!

I remember one time when we went on bivouac, it poured down rain. In the evening after the rain, they built a big bonfire. We had beer and watermelon. Kocur brought his accordion and I taught the guys how to do the Virginia Reel, one of them also did the Russian Saber Dance. It was fun!

When our outfit shipped out to Camp Cooke and got settled in, we went on hikes in the sand. Our first hike was to be 10 miles, skip two days, then 20 miles, skip another two days, then 30 miles. The tendons in the back of my legs got very sore after the 10 mile hike. I asked Sergeant Reid if I could forget the 20 mile hike to rest my legs for the 30 miles. He said I was goldbricking and had to go on the 20 mile hike. While talking to Klickstein, the CO clerk, in the shower that evening, he expounded on how to diagnose appendicitis. I remembered the symptoms and half way through the 20 mile hike, I faked it and good! When I jumped up in the air Klickstein yelled: "it's Martin and it's his appendix!" They rushed me to the hospitals surgery ward where I faked it again (that was a mistake!). The patient across the isle from me said they brought someone in awhile back with possible appendix symptoms.

The doctor's accused him of goldbricking and sent him back to his outfit, only to have him come back again, the next day with a ruptured appendix. In spite of my protests and pleading, THEY KEPT ME FOR 2 MONTHS!

The review board then said that I could stay for another month, go on limited service, or go back to my outfit. I wanted to go back to my outfit, just to spite them! When I got back, Sergeant Melton said that I could lie around the barracks for a few days to recuperate from my surgery. I told him I appreciated his concern. That evening I was caught! Sergeant Melton wanted to see my scar. I told him I was bashful and would prefer not to expose my privates. He said, "LET ME SEE YOUR SCAR!" I tried to get by with showing him and old hernia scar, but he said "That's on the wrong side!" After realizing I did not have an operation, I got every 'crappy' detail they had and some they just thought up.

We shipped out to Europe on the U.S.S. Alexandria. The toilets in the Head were unique, the seats in the stalls were built over a long trough with water rushing through it. Every morning after breakfast when guys were seated on the toilets, someone in the first stall would light a wad of toilet paper and drop it into the rapids rushing below. You could see the guys jump up and cuss as the burning paper shot along the trough.

We landed in France and were temporarily stationed at camp Old Gold. The damp winter air made us cold all the time. The coal miners had gone on strike back home which kept us from getting coke to burn. We had to burn our rifle oil, tent pegs and cot slaves to keep warm. I was bitter against the miners.

Our water supply was interesting. It was purified with halazone tablets, which made the water taste like Clorox and Listerine. It was rationed and part of our ration consisted of 2/3s canteen cup of water, with which to brush our teeth, shave, take a sponge bath and wash our socks. If we did not do it in that order, we had a problem!

I remember we shipped out in tiny little 40x8 boxcars from WW I, 40 men or eight horses. They were nice, they only put 36 men in our boxcar.

After we got established on the Rhine, Lt. Brooks called the 1st Platoon together and informed us that orders came down to send a reconnaissance patrol across the river. He volunteered to lead it.

He said that he expected all nine volunteers to come from the 1st Platoon. After one helluva pep talk, he said that he would let the first nine men who raised their hands go, the rest would have to stay. I wanted to be sure to be one of the first nine to raise their hands, so my hand shot up! I looked around to see and I WAS IT! Finally, Lansford and Burkett raised their hands. I do not remember who else went, other then Meyers. There were twelve men including the two engineers. They gave us some training, mainly on firing the 'grease-gun'. We were to search a fixed perimeter and hopefully bring back a prisoner.

We blackened our faces, rolled up our sleeves; put on an inflatable life belt with two inflating capsules. In total darkness the men got on each side of the boat and started down the bank. I decided to get under the boat to help hold it up. Halfway down the bank they started setting the boat down to rest, both capsules in my life belt burst and inflated before I could grab on to someone's leg to get out. Someone grabbed my collar and kicked the fire out of me. I think it was Lt. Brooks.

After crossing, we disembarked, bellied up the bank with our sleeves rolled up, through about an inch of crude oil residue, then we bellied through a thick patch of nettles, which really burned and itched. The engineers cut through the concertina wire, as we stepped over the trip wire each man took the hand of the man behind him and placed it on the trip wire. We crept into the fixed perimeter that was outlined for us and could not find a soul. We were all greased up and no place to go! I believe if we had seen a rabbit, we would have shot it! We came back empty handed. Although we did not encounter enemy fire, Lt. Brooks said that we would be the first ten men in the Division to receive the Combat Infantry Badge. The majority of the men in the 86th Division were 18 and 19 year old teenagers, which made the average age of the entire 17,000 man division 22 ½ years. We were the youngest age group division in the entire allied armies. Our company had three rifle platoons consisting of 40 men each. In combat, each rifleman was issued 384 rounds of ammunition plus 4 hand grenades. To dispose of it we had to shoot it or be court-martialed. We were like a bunch of 'ornery' teenagers on Halloween night!

All I know about splitting the Rhur Pocket is what happened right in front of me. We were on 2 ½ ton trucks, I didn't see any tanks or tank destroyers. They said a German soldier waved a white flag, the truck stopped and was hit by a panzerfaust, killing some of our men. I was told the Recon Car went through and spotted some ambushes. We were told our trucks would drive through FAST while the men seated on the outside would fire at the windows and at anything that moved while the men in the middle would reload. I understand that, for our little escapade, Goeble's propaganda radio charged the 86th Division with being "Roosevelt's S.S. Troops!"

The tanks finally arrived, but had to pull back at dusk because they could not see in the dark. At dark, it becomes a foot soldier's SPEARHEAD as we went by a Tiger Tank in the middle of the road, I hurriedly felt the gun muzzle on it, and checked the caliber of the machine guns. Someone in 2nd Platoon got curious and looked inside and found 5 German Soldiers just being very quiet. After capturing them someone dropped an incendiary grenade in it and held up the column for 15 minutes while the ammo went off like the 4th of July!

After dark, it was our 1st Platoons turn to take the spearhead. We moved up and after a while, the column stopped and word was passed back; "Who can operate a "bazooka'?" I said, "I can operate a 'bazooka'." Word went back, "Martin can operate a 'bazooka, send Martin up." I thought, "Wait a minute, I'm not the only one whose had 'bazooka' training!" but I had to go on up. The Lt. handed me a folding bazooka. I had never seen a folding bazooka, and in the dark, I could not see that one. The Lt. said, "See that thing up there, I don't know if it's a tank or half track, just KNOCK IT OUT! Burgchardt will load and tap." I said "Lt., they might not know we're here and if they do, they don't know how many. If I fire and miss, the back flash will light up the whole battalion, they might knock out half the battalion before I could get reloaded. He said, "Good thinking Martin, me and Brownie will slip up on them." They moved up and after firing their rifles, I heard cleated shoes running, an engine started and the thing took off!

We moved on up and under 'blackout' conditions we saw two red lights ahead. At first, they appeared stationary, then one moved down in a semi-circle, then the other moved down then back up. We thought they were signaling, we moved up slowly and almost ran into them. They were two displaced persons smoking cigarettes. They started yelling

"NIX NAZI!" and one of them shined a flashlight on his face to show us he was not a Nazi! It was a box light with the switch next to the bulb. Someone grabbed the light, covered the bulb (and switch) with their left hand and tried to beat the light out with their right hand. The other displaced person very helpfully turned his lights on to show them the switch. Somebody knocked that light out of his hand and chased the light over an embankment trying to stomp it out. The situation was comical! We sent the displaced persons behind our lines, with their flashlights!

Since it was late, and with little opposition, it was decided that we were to leave our Platoon on the spearhead until we reached the outskirts of Hagen. We finally arrived at this great big stone house. We hurried inside, threw some of our equipment on the various beds to claim them for ourselves. Lt. Brooks wanted the house for a Platoon Command Post. Also, without our knowledge, the higher ups wanted it for a Company Command Post, a Battalion Command Post, a Regimental Command Post and a Division Command Post. When the tank destroyers started forming a semi circle around the house, I thought "Man those T.D. guys sure think a lot of our platoon!" While the T.D.'s were getting into position, we heard something coming down the road. Someone said, "Something's coming, sounds like a tank, we had better try to stop it!" Thaxton said, "I'll stop it and trots out in the middle of the road at 'port-arms'. Someone grabbed him and took him to cover. Then one of the men said, "I gotta crap, what'll I do?" Sergeant Melton said "CRAP", and the poor guy squats right under the muzzle of a tank destroyer just as it zeroed in on the tank coming toward us. When the tank destroyer fired, the guy started crying and said, "I can't stop 'crapping', now what'll I do?" Sergeant Melton said, "Just keep right on 'crapping," and the rest of us started diving for cover.

After things died down a bit, Meixner came over and told me that he had an odd experience. He said that after being relieved of guard duty, he went in to sleep and found someone in his bed. He said he grabbed the guy by the collar and belt, shook him and said, "I put my stuff on this bed to claim it! Who is this?" He said, "This is General Melasky, who are you?" I said, "Just one of your boys, General" and slipped out.

When I awoke the next morning, I went into the living room and Van Dielen came through asking, "Who can drive a truck?" I said, "I can drive a truck." I thought, ORDINANCE HERE I COME! Although I had never been in the driver's seat of a 2 ½ ton truck, Masclay said, "I can drive a truck." Van Dielen said, "The captain wants someone to bring the trucks up so the men can get their packs and be more comfortable. I said, "What happened to the regular drivers?" He said, "They deserted the trucks." I opened the front door and it looked like it was 'raining sideways' in both directions. Lots of tracers going both ways! We bellied out and up the road. When we reached a point across from the trucks, I yelled over to Masclay that they ought to court-martial the drivers for deserting their trucks. One of the drivers stuck his head out from behind the front wheel of his truck and said, "I would desert the damn thing if the Krauts would let us out from behind this wheel." I said, "The Captain wants you all to bring the trucks up to that stone house with the men's packs, so they can get more comfortable." He said, "If someone will start it, I might send it up there, but I ain't about to drive it, not now anyhow!" We bellied our way back and told Van Dielen they would bring the trucks up soon as they got out of the line of fire.

Later, we expected a counter attack and dug in two-man foxholes. We ran rope lines between the foxholes to keep us awake. I remember someone jerked my line and told me Roosevelt had died. It was a sad and questioning moment.

We regrouped, then started 'mopping up'. Riding tanks and tank destroyers, until they ran out of fuel, then walking. The first night, expecting a counter attack, we dug in. It did not come, so we pulled out before daylight, and for the next three days and nights we walked, with only a ten-minute break every hour.

I remember coming to the forks in a road. We stopped. Lt. Brooks came up front and asked the lead scout why he stopped? The lead scout said, "There aren't any signs and I don't have a map, so I stopped because I didn't know which way to go." The Lt. told everyone within hearing distance, and I still remember it, "Men, I want this to be a lesson to you. All your life you will be coming to forks in the road and you will not know which way to go. There will be no signs and no maps, but dam-it, go one way or the other, but do not stop. When you stop you begin defeating your purpose and you will hold up many people behind you. Here one man held up a battalion." Lesson learned.

We continued marching and at night, I did not dare sit down during our 10-minute break because I could not get up when we started out again. We learned to listen to the footsteps ahead of us and sleep while we walked. In my sleep, I walked out into a field. They had to come after me. Janitschek dreamed he was falling off a tank and he fell over a hillside.

We finally stopped at a farm village and bunked in. I went up to a bedroom, lit a candle and saw an old man in a double bed. I took off my jacket and shoes, hung my helmet on the foot of the bed and crawled in with the old man. I pulled his hot water bottle over with my feet as he slept. Meixner came in and joined us by crawling in on the other side of the man. We got into a foot fight over the hot water bottle, which woke up the old man. Not realizing American troops were within miles of the place, he sat up, looked at me and Meixner, then at our helmets, yelled something in German, climbed over the foot of the bed and we never saw him again.

The next morning I went outside and Sergeant Melton was frying eggs from a crate. I asked him to fry me some eggs. He told me he would stop frying when I told him to. I ate 23 eggs.

We finally got three days of R & R. I heard that the mail clerk, the bugler and one of the cooks went deer hunting, brought back a deer and a German prisoner. I heard he killed one German soldier, captured the other and had him carry the deer back.

The fuel supplies and ordinance finally caught up with us. We headed south, riding the tank destroyers. It had snowed and rained. We had our raincoats on under our rifle belts. One of the guys, Randall, I believe was very skinny and had to bunch his belt up in front and tie it with a rope. He laid too long on the tank destroyer's exhaust manifold and his ammunition started exploding. The bottom half of his raincoat dropped around his ankles while he hurriedly untied his rope and slung the dancing belt into the ditch. Everyone else hit the dirt and supply Sergeant yelled, "Get your canteen, get your canteen, we're short on canteens!" It was hilarious!

I remember hurrying through this farm village searching out the enemy. As we hurried through this barn, Van Dielen grabbed a hen off the nest, was squeezing it and yelling "lay, damn you, lay". At that moment, eggs outranked the enemy.

In the late afternoon, we stopped at this house in a small farm village. Sergeant Melton told me to inform the German Lady we would be spending the night. She and her family could stay in one room of the house. I informed her and she in turn pinched my cheek and said (in German), "Oh such a little child!" She said that she would allow us to stay, but I would have to take a bath and let her wash my clothes. Unfortunately, Sergeant Melton caught the gist of the conversation and thought it was a good idea. The other guys drug the tub to the middle of the yard and then filled it with warm water. She brought out men's civilian clothes, a towel and soap. They gave her my clothes and I took a bath. I wanted to quit being an interpreter for our squad.

We headed south and stopped at Berghausen, at the border of Germany and Austria on the Inn River. The 'higher ups' decided that our 1st Platoon should remain in Berghausen and guard the only bridge at this point, separating the two countries from possible sabotage. In addition, we were to set up a 'check point' and temporary military government. All went well for one day, then the liberated Serb and Yugoslav POWs started rounding up German soldier prisoners and bringing them in. We improvised a makeshift stockade. While Meixner and I were guarding it, we used Hitler's policy of 'Divide and Conquer!' We took all personal possessions away from the prisoners and gave them to the other prisoners. The dissention we created kept them from organizing a breakout.

The war finally ended! We were relocated to Vernheim for a few days. I learned that my older brother with the 28th Division was in Kaiserslautern. I went to visit him and was told he was in Vernheim to see his brother (which was me). We finally got together.

We shipped out to stateside, got a 30-day delay in route home, then to Camp Gruber, OK. My hometown buddy was graduating from aviation cadets at Childers Army Air Base, TX, near Camp Gruber. I went to the base and visited with my buddy. Just as I was to return to Camp Gruber, they dropped the atomic bomb. I figured the war was over! My buddy said that it would be nice if I could stay over for his graduation. I figured Hell, the war's over, and besides I am on an army air base. They will not fuss at me. "WRONG!" I was court-martialed for being four days AWOL and shipped to the Philippines with my outfit.

Aboard ship, every evening after dinner, I would read a letter I had obtained from one of the cadets, written from his wife. It was an EXTREMELY LUSTFUL LETTER and the guys loved to hear me read it to them.

I boxed exhibition bouts, featherweight class, aboard ship. I sometimes cheated by contacting my opponent before the fight and inferring I had many more fights than he did and if he would just let me win, I wouldn't hurt him. Sometimes it worked!

While we were in the port of Batangas, Luzon, James Murry showed me a carton of cigarettes. He then opened the carton and showed me it was filled with blocks of wood. He said he was going to "Take a Gook" with his "Cigarettes". We got into camp and I saw him make the trade. After the trade, both he and the Filipino ran in opposite directions. I stopped him and saw that he had traded his wooden blocks for worthless Japanese invasion currency! (Talk about Arabs trading hats in the desert!)

Garrison duty got boring. Division Headquarters transferred me to the M.P. Platoon to get me on their boxing team. I boxed for division headquarters, but lost the division featherweight championship. Two Indians on the boxing team thought I was pretty smart, so they asked if I would join them in business when we got home. I felt complimented and asked what type of business they were pursuing? They said "HIJACKING FISHING BOATS, beyond the 12 mile limit, anything goes, and there's good money in it!" I declined their invitation.

Highlights of my postwar life:

- Came home from the Army, and attended the University of Chicago for two years, was educated quit a bit.
- Sold encyclopedias, worked in the Post Office, became a Scoutmaster, did landscape designing, did roadside development for the West Virginia Turnpike.

- Got married just six weeks after meeting a lady who later became my bride, became a photo-engraver, sold real estate for eight years, became a real estate appraiser and then joined HUD-FHA
- Had a heart attack in '68, In '69 got a whitewater kayak and ran the rapids for about 3 years til I knocked a hole in it, (I was glad), went skiing and played volleyball.
- In '72 my wife and I divorced, no children.
- In '76 I bought a condo at the Snowshoe Ski Resort in West Virginia.
- In December of '79 I married Judy who is the most beautiful person, inside and out.
- In '80 HUD-FHA had a reduction in force and retired me early, they put me back to work in '85 as a Review Appraiser, (appraising appraiser's appraisals).
- In '87 I sold my condominium, quit appraising and had quadruple by-pass surgery.
- After dislocating my shoulder and getting a torn rotator cuff, I have let up on my skiing.
- My wife and I live in Belle, WV

Crossing My Rubicon
by Emil (343rd Inf) and Ruth Treeson

Emil Treson (above) and Glen J. Miller

The men of the 86th division Infantry forces slugged forward on another chilly, early, gray March morning, advancing deeper into the heartland of Germany. The tired men were almost swallowed by the ground fog that snaked its way among the trees. As we approached the footbridge over the rushing water of the Danube River, the fog became denser.

Suddenly a heavyset pale, wide bottomed first sergeant appeared in front of my squad, and yelled at a young teenage soldier from Alabama, "Hey You," and pointed to a loaded wooden communication cable reel, ordering him to move get over there. Then turning towards me, he yelled, "Hey, hey."

I replied in my most intelligent manner, "You mean, me, me?"

"Yeah, yeah, I don't mean Suzy. Get your butt over to that cable reel."

"Yes Sir," I said and dragged my tired feet to where he pointed, not knowing what he'd want me to do next. I almost scratched my head trying to figure out what this sergeant was doing here now, as I've never seen him before, but I used my usual response to military authority, passive resistance.

He raised his voice once again addressing the southern soldier, "Grab that short pipe length and stick it. You know where."

Instinctively, the young soldier inserted the short pipe length through the center hole of the reel. The sergeant ordered me to grasp the rear end of the pipe so we could both carry it. We joined a group of twelve other soldiers, and began walking, carrying the reel towards the footbridge. As we approached the start of the footbridge, a barrage of fire came towards us from the other side. We hit the ground, while our side returned the fire. A couple of soldiers with cameras started to pop up and down, taking pictures. They were army photographers, documenting our outfit running across the footbridge under fire.

Suddenly, there was a lull in the firing from both sides. Someone yelled, "Go," and both of us along with others rose in unison and started running across this footbridge. I was in the rear, holding on to the center pipe with my right hand, which left my left hand free to swing.

I had slung my BAR (Browning Automatic Rifle) over my left shoulder. The enemy opened up with intense firing just as we reached the center of the bridge. I felt a very sharp pain in the palm of my left hand. Did a large, poisonous snake or a bat bite me? My mind raced thinking of ways to lessen my pain.

I dipped my left shoulder quickly to relieve the pain. As I did so, my heavy automatic rifle began to slide down my left arm and while I attempted to hold on to it, I lost my balance. Now I struggled to regain secure footing. I figured that if I pulled on the pipe with my right hand, chances are I may still go over the side of the bridge pulling my carrying companion along with me. I knew it would be difficult if not impossible to swim against the river current, fully armed, and in winter uniforms. Besides the thought of the frigid winter river water concerned me.

As a former life guard, I'm a reasonably strong swimmer, therefore I figured that if I had to end up in the river, it would be best if I wasn't encumbered by the additional weight of the fully loaded cable reel and my carrying companion, who may not be a swimmer. The next thing I knew, I was under water, looking up to the light above the surface of the water.

I needed air. My arms pulled in an awkward breaststroke and I broke through and gasped several deep gulps of the moist cool air.

I was facing up stream, eyes focused on the footbridge, when I recognized the short, stocky soldier from my company's heavy weapons fourth platoon, an Italian American guy, and a good poker player, who wore glasses. Now he was squatting, balanced on his toes, holding on to the guide wire with his left hand over his head, while reaching towards me with his right arm. "Grab my hand!" He shouted repeatedly.

His was a very courageous, generous offer, but I recognized that he was risking his life. Had I accepted his generous offer, I'd have had to expend my limited energy and swim a very hard ten feet upstream, before I could reach his outstretched hand. Then too, had I reached him I'd be completely exhausted. My dead weight may have proven too heavy for him, and instead of being rescued; both of us would end up locked in a death embrace.

I could do nothing else but take the chance and swim for my life by myself. The lose chinstrap on my helmet caused it to come off, by itself, and as I dipped my shoulder to lessen the pain, my heavy rifle slid off my left arm.

In order to survive, I had to get rid of my loaded cartridge belt, which was securely fastened about my waist. I made a conscious effort not to panic. After I took a deep breath, I went under again, and grasping both sides of my buckle, struggled to release it. Securely holding the left side with my left hand, my right hand rotated the right side of the buckle 90 degrees. I succeeded in releasing the belt and let it drop to the bottom of the river. Then I started back towards its surface. Breaking through to the surface, I looked for the two photographers. Seeing them told me which side of the river to swim for, and I made for that riverbank.

One of the photographers ran down stream to keep pace with me. Because the river was so fast, the photographer couldn't keep pace with me. He paused to catch his breath, and then he continued to walk rapidly down stream trying to keep up. Still, the current took me far ahead of him. In the end I reached the embankment, and breathed the moist, cool air thankfully. Then exhausted, I stretched on the ground.

It took some time, before that photographer reached me. Trying to help me breathe, he grabbed hold of my belt and started to move my body lifting it up and down. His actions made it worse, and I told him to stop.

After a while, I managed to get up on my feet. It was at that point that I became conscious of the pain in my left palm. I was shivering with cold, as well. We walked back slowly along the riverbank to the start of the footbridge. There I hoped to catch a ride in a Jeep back to the battalion aid station. We arrived at the bridge joining the other photographer and crouched among the trees because of enemy had resumed firing. Occasionally soldiers crossed the bridge to advance against the enemy, while the army photographers continued documenting our side advancing against the enemy.

A platoon with a first Lt. in charge approached the footbridge. He drew his big 45-caliber pistol, and promptly jumped into a foxhole, as he waved his men forward across the bridge. Only when the last man crossed safely, did he determine that it was safe to come out of his hiding place and follow his men.

At his show of cowardice, the three of us expressed our collective disgust. I shook my head in wonder, "How did our side get this far with such leadership?"

Next, a Jeep stopped a good half-mile from the bridge. Both the driver and its passenger, an officer got out of the vehicle. The officer took out a pair of binoculars to observe the activities around the bridge. I shouted for them to wait for me, and walked to meet them. When I requested a ride to the battalion aid station, the uncertain driver deferred to the officer. At first, that worthy individual refused my humble request. It didn't matter to him that I made a pitiful figure, shivering in a soaking wet uniform, with blood dripping from my left palm. But he changed his mind, when I advanced towards him, anger clearly showing on my face. I thus reached the goodness of his heart, because he promptly changed his mind and told me to jump in.

We arrived at the aid station. It was located in a German farmhouse, taken over by our battalion. The sight of many pale soldiers lining every inch of the floor, stretched out on narrow cots and field-operating tables greeted me as I entered the room. Some of them were having their bleeding wounds sown up, while others were being fed intravenously. Some of the soldiers lay unconscious, not moving. I did not know how many of them were already dead. Doctors and medics moved rapidly, attending to the most seriously wounded.

Seeing their dire predicament, I decided to treat and bandage the wounded palm of my left hand by myself. Then I went in search of a dry winter uniform, a rifle, a helmet, and some ammunition. Just before I left I noticed a uniform with suspenders and an empty cartridge belt lying abandoned in a corner of the room. I changed into the dry clothes, and feeling more comfortable, put on the cartridge belt and went outside.

There by the side of the road next to a puddle of blood, I saw a helmet, its liner, and two grenades. I took them along. Fortunately, a Jeep picked me up, and dropped me off near the footbridge. I was concerned for my life, but I wanted to rejoin my outfit to help my Division to advance against the enemy. As I approached the footbridge, I thought that I was completely alone. Suddenly, seemingly out of nowhere I heard, "It's too damn freezing in this damp hole." I discovered two soldiers hiding in a foxhole, and called down to ask them if the area on the other side of the bridge had been secured. They did not respond at first, but then, a hesitant head appeared. After telling me that it was safe to cross over, the soldier dropped back into the foxhole in a hurry, while the other guy bitterly complained of being crowded.

Before deciding to proceed, I tried to evaluate the situation for myself. Except for the sounds of birds in the trees, the murmur of the river, and the rustling of the leaves, all seemed quiet on the Eastern Front. Armed with my two grenades, which I had securely fastened to my suspenders, I decided to make the run across the bridge

I was in the middle of the bridge, when the heavens exploded with enemy fire. I had two choices: go back into the drink again, or run back like hell. Bullets, whistled past my head, and tore into the bridge and the river below. I was nineteen, and doubtful of making twenty. Adrenalin pumping, I ran like hell back to the safe side of the bridge. As I ran, a new hale of bullets, this time from the friendly side, covered my retreat.

The enemy fire ceased, but I didn't stop to look until I got back to our end of the bridge and hit the ground. Then I saw an undermanned squad of brave, American soldiers firing at the enemy, with others calling frantically for back up. This squad didn't begin to match the numbers of the enemy. Now, sixty years later, I have no doubt that these young American men saved my life. My only regret is that I never learned their names. I would very much like to thank them.

I did my part, when I unwittingly drew enemy fire. That's how I exposed the enemy's position, their 88 artillery gun mounted on a flat bed railroad car, along with its crew, and a considerable stash of ammunition. Once their position was exposed, our Colonel Bloomquist knew where to direct a large enough force to put them out of action. When it was all over, I had still to cross the bridge, but first I caught my breath, and ate a chocolate bar from my meal rations. Only then, did I make my third and final successful attempt at crossing the bridge. The first thing to greet me after crossing over was the wooden communication reel with its full complement of cable. There it was lying abandoned on its side, its carrying pipe sticking up through the center.

When I finally caught up with my company's headquarters it was far from the battlefront. I attempted to report in to our beloved First Sergeant Roach, affectionately called "cockroach." He kept me waiting for several hours, which I put to good use by sleeping on the headquarters floor. When I was allowed to report for duty, and explained what happened to me, he reflected deeply, stroked his chin, and sweetly asked, "Do you want a medal?"

This was the first time I saw him this close to the front line. Besides, when I remembered how he beat one of the men in our company for returning a few hours late from visiting his family, and that was only a few days before we all shipped overseas from our Boston area camp, I was not surprised that he didn't tuck me into bed and croon me a lullaby.

"Alea iacta est'

I never had a chance to personally thank the Italian American soldier from my company who risked his life to help me. I wanted to reach out to him, as he reached out to me. Sixty plus years later, I got the chance to do so, when I received a letter from the man who witnessed me falling into the water as he walked behind me on the bridge. Glenn J. Miller wrote to advise me that it was Moody T. Caperna, who despite wearing a heavy and awkward mortar vest with six rounds in it, risked his life, trying to save me. I was able to find Moody and his present address with the help of the internet site, "Anywho." After I thanked him by telephone, we corresponded and recalled those times.

I dedicate my story to all the men of our outfit, who lost their lives, and to my friends, Stan and Sid, my Bronx neighbors, who were killed on the frontlines in Cologne, shortly before our outfit relieved theirs. I would also like to remember my childhood friend, an infantry medic, Murray, who suffered a bullet wound one inch above his heart. He was hit during the height of a battle, while attending the severely wounded on both sides. Lastly, I dedicate this story to a child, who was the only member of her family to survive of the holocaust. Through her writing she was able to capture the living spirit of those whom she loved and who perished.

How I Skipped the Pacific Theater
by David Moore 342nd K Co.

I was going up a back street in Berglern (Bavaria) with PFC Don Carter when I was shot. As I fell, I saw the German soldier who shot me. I was told later that Don was able to wound and capture him.

The bullet broke my left tibia. I played dead for a while, dreading a follow-on bullet. After about 15 minutes, I rolled over to reach my rifle and got out my medical kit. There was almost no blood because the tibia is just under the skin. I took my disinfection pill, got out a Beretta handgun I had liberated, made sure I could fire it, and waited. After what in retrospect lasted about an hour, one of our medics and Don Carter showed up with the German family who lived in the house and I was laid out on a mattress on the first floor. My German hosts gave me a bowl of soup. After about three hours a medic showed up with a guard and four German prisoners with a litter. By this time the town was ours, and a number of prisoners were grouped on one side of the farmstead with jeep-mounted .50 caliber machine guns monitoring the scene.

After changing the dressing on my wound, I was taken to the Mittel Isar Canal, crossed by boat, then to the 37th Evacuation Hospital. I had heard that a childhood friend was in this hospital so I asked if John Coffland worked there. John was the son of good friends of my folks, and I knew him well. While the surgeon was debriding my wound, John and I had our reunion. I was equipped with a long leg cast and put on a cot for the night. The next day I was able to write a short note to my parents telling them about being wounded and about my meeting with John. This letter was the first word his parents had heard from him for a month or two.

The next stop was Rheims, France. I was there on the night of May 8th when the Germans surrendered and tracer bullets laced the sky. The next day a C-47 hospital aircraft took me to Great Malvern, England. I became more mobile, learned to use crutches and helped other patients write letters, and waited. The next trip was by rail to Glasgow, Scotland, where we were housed in a school gym. I remember how light it was. At 11:00 p.m. you could read by light coming through the window.

From Prestwick Air Base in Scotland I took a C-54 hospital plane which stopped at Reflavik, Iceland, and Gander, Newfoundland to refuel en route to Mitchell Field, Long Island, NY. Before landing on June 18, 1945, I must have flown over the first ships to bring troops home from Europe, which carried my 86th Blackhawk Division comrades. After dining with celebrities at Billy Rose's Diamond Horseshow (in pajamas and military bathrobes) I had medical visits in Tennessee, Ft. Custer Rehab Hospital outside Battle Creek, Michigan and a 45-day leave at home in Cadiz, OH before I got my ruptured duck at Camp Atterbury, IN on Easter Monday, April 22, 1946. It was time to return to MIT to pick up my education where I had left it to go to war.

The Best Job In The Army I
by Roland E. Hopkins, Maj USA (Ret)

Roland E. "Hop" Hopkins (top left) and fellow Artillery spotter pilots

The end of the war was announced yesterday and as an artillery liaison pilot of a Piper Cub (L-4) spotting targets for a battalion of 155 mm howitzers it ended for me the best job in the Army, as I had no peacetime mission. So I asked my fellow pilot, Lt. Steve Lowry, if he'd like to join me in flying over to Adolf Hitler's home and Alpine retreat at Berchtesgarden. Sounded like a good idea to him, so off we flew. Fifteen minutes later we arrived at Der Fuhrer's hideaway, the Eagle's Nest, and looked in vain for a suitable place to land. We were trained to land in small, tight places, but this landscape was now covered with rubble from Air Force bombings and wine-filled French occupation troops. Finally we found a small pasture about a mile west of Hitler's place which offered no place to take off from, but we decided to land now and worry about our departure later. As we looked for a place to hide our little plane a German farmer armed with a three-pronged pitch fork appeared. He knew no English and we only knew one German word, which we used. "Verboten" we said as we patted our .45's and pointed to the plane. He got the picture and left. We headed to the road to hitch a ride when we suddenly realized that we'd better think of a way to find our plane after sightseeing. Drawing on our Boy Scout training we built a pile of baseball-sized field stones beside the road and tied a handkerchief to an evergreen above it. Just as we finished our navigational aid, an old Dodge command car with a French flag on the bumper came rattling up the road. We stopped it and found inside a French General who agreed to give us a lift to Hitler's compound. We were constantly saluted (because of the General Officer) by French troops, most of whom were feeling no pain. This caused us to wonder where these troops were getting their wine, and we shortly spotted a fenced area from which drunken French soldiers emerged.

Entering Hitler's bombed-out villa we saw through the rubble the second story balcony where Hitler had posed for photos that I had seen on the cover of Life Magazine. After working our way across steel girders we reached the balcony to take pictures of each other with arms and forefingers outstretched in the way Hitler posed during for his halcyon days. We then moved next door to a bombed building which I assumed to be Hitler's library. Why? Because there was a 6 or 7-foot tall pyramid of books blasted from shelves on the sides into the middle of the room. I climbed to the top and there found a rather large book with artist's pictures bound with a leather cover and gilt-edged pages. I felt this volume might be important and interesting so I liberated it as a souvenir. Then it was off to the wine cellar.

Emerging with armloads of what turned out to be vin very ordinaire, we spotted an 86th Div truck. When the driver told us that his passenger was Chief of Staff Col. Jones, we made a quick deal to hide a dozen bottles of wine under the truck tarp . We'd split the loot with him at his motor pool at 8 the next morning. He agreed and we split.

So at about 2:30 p.m. we walked out of the compound, each nursing a bottle of wine, to look for our airplane. We found it OK and no pitchfork-carrying German. Just as I had put our plane onto that too small pasture I decided to take it off or we would both die happy from drinking Hitler's wine. Really it was a cinch, with a slight downhill grade, when you run out of ground you are in the air. It's the very best job in the U.S. Army!

The Best Job in the Army, Part II: Visit to Switzerland

Our war with Germany was over and we Blackhawks were slated to return home en route to the Pacific to take on Japan. But wait! Too many of us were moving towards Le Havre, the exodus had to be slowed, so the 86th Div. Air Sections had to halt and set up camp. I quickly decided this was my chance to fly one of our "Cubs" to Switzerland to buy some stamps for my collection. So, I made out an operation order for an area on the Swiss border. One of my sergeants said that he would like to come along and I said O.K.. We prepared well by taking two extra cans of gas and maps of the area.

After 2 ½ hours our tank was about empty, so when we spotted a small group of Army trucks we landed in a nearby pasture. It turned out the personnel in our trucks were French, and they refused to give us gas. All hell broke out in me and I backed up my demand for gas by saying that if they refused I'd see to it that all U.S. equipment in the area would be immediately reclaimed by our Engineers, who were just a mile away. They saw how mad I was, so I got my gas and left.

After about eight hours of flying in our L-4 we were tired and evening was upon us. So we headed for the closest U.S.A.F base shown on our map in Dijon, France. There we spent the night in nice quarters and partook of a few drinks. Up early, got gas, made out an operations order giving Geneva, Switzerland, about 30 miles to the south, as our destination. So away we go and in less than an hour flew by the Geneva airport, our intended destination, so I could see Lake Geneva and all the League of Nations buildings. After taking a dozen photos with the camera I kept under my seat, we headed back to the large Geneva airport and taxied in the direction of the control tower.

A civilian gentleman walked out to meet us and asked us to park our plane and come to the office. This we did and another man pushed our airplane into a hanger. A nice gesture, I thought. Upon reaching the office building, we were offered wine and told that we would have to be interrogated by the military police, who were on their way. They soon arrived and I was questioned as to my authority for landing at Geneva. It struck me that we might be in some kind of trouble. After a half hour of silly questions, I asked how soon I could go into Geneva to see some stamp dealers. I am told that we had to wait for the Swiss Air Commandant to arrive from another city. So more wine and waiting. Finally the official shows up in the prettiest pure white aircraft with a huge red cross on its tail. He asks the same type questions and wants to confiscate my camera. I refuse but say they can have the film in it. They agree and there are more questions and wine, but we cannot go into the city. Lunchtime arrived and we are fed very nice sandwiches from the nearby city we wanted to visit.

Finally, about 2 p.m. the Swiss official announced his decision: We are giving you your plane back, but I am going to stand right here and watch you take off to the west (German border) and "don't you ever come back."

We thanked him, took off, landed in about an hour on territory occupied by U.S. Engineers who were surprised to see us. We filled our 12-gal. gas tank plus two extra cans, had a snack and about 4 p.m. away we go. We figured the distance to get to our destination and realized we couldn't make it by nightfall. Now, one does not fly unlighted small planes after dark. Regardless, we fly straight north and as the sky gradually darkens, lights shine up from the towns and villages and along the north-south rivers, which helped out navigation. Finally, after 10:00 p.m., I locate Weinsheim and our landing area. So I buzzed the strip and circled around a couple of times. My aircraft mechanic shows up in a Jeep, drives the length of the strip, turns around, douses the headlights and turns on his flashlight, partly shielded by his fingers, and we make a perfect landing. Too tired to poop!

Please remember: we don't fly at night. We are not trained or equipped for that sort of thing!

After we get staged in about ten days, a messenger arrives with an urgent message for me to report to Col. Jones, our division's chief of staff. So away I go to see him. I salute, he doesn't return it.

"Hopkins, did you go to Switzerland while we were in Germany?"
"Yes sir."
"What did you do that for?"
"Because I wanted to go, sir."
"Don't you know about Switzerland's strict neutrality?"
"Yes, sir," I said, "I do now."

About this time I notice a stack of papers about 2 to 3 inches thick in front of the colonel. I ask if these papers are about my Swiss visit. "Hell, yes," he shouts. I ask if they are copies of pictures I took while flying over Switzerland. "Hell yes," he says

"May I see them, sir?"

"Sure."

"May I have several?"

"Hell no, they must be returned with my endorsement through channels with other endorsements to the Swiss government.

I said, "Sir, I have a copy in my foot locker of the operation order that I received from the ops officer at our US Air Force base in Dijon, France, to fly into Geneva. Would that be of any help?

"Hell, yes, go get it!" I did and that was the end of the affair.

Roland E. Hopkins, Maj USA (Ret) spent 31 years in Army and National Guard, logged more than 2,500 hours flying Piper Cubs and L-19 (Bird Dog).

My Buddy—General Pope
by Dave Herold 342nd L Co.

George van Wyck Pope was more than a General and Assistant Division Commander of the 86th Division. He was also a 'buddy' to many of the troops in his command. Following are some recollections by several troops under his command that illustrate the human qualities of this fine professional soldier.

Tom Boles, Co. I, 343rd Inf reports:

I was drafted in 1942, and sent to Camp Howse in Jan. 1943. After a few weeks, I volunteered for an easy job. After finishing this, I sat down in the warm sun coming through the window and fell asleep. When I looked up after a tap on the shoulder, I saw a star on the shoulder of the officer standing in front of me. I jumped up very startled and he told me to sit down and tell him where I was from. I responded: "Thomas F Boles from Liberal, Kansas." He wanted to know where that was and I explained it was a small town in southwest Kansas.

A few years later in 1945 I was walking up a country road in the Ruhr Pocket in Germany. A jeep pulled up beside me and General Pope says "Kansas—get in". We visited about the troops and the food for about ten minutes. The jeep stopped and I got out. I was very honored that he remembered me. Col. Baumer came running over and asked if I gave him a good report. I replied: "I'm no dummy!"

That was the last time I saw General Pope, but I'll remember him forever.

Bob Bookbinder, former President of the 86th Division Association recalls:

It was during late 1944 and I had just joined the 86th at Camp San Luis Obispo, CA. I was a 'fresh' 2nd Lieutenant, just out of the Officer's Candidate School at Ft. Benning, GA, and my assignment was that of Platoon Leader of the Ammunition and Pioneer Platoon of Headquarters Co., 1st Battalion, 343rd Infantry. During one of our training exercises at Camp San Luis Obispo, I was directed to participate in an operation where I was to lead my platoon up one of the many hills and "capture" it. It was during this exercise, as we crawled up this hill, that I noted one member of the platoon crawling somewhat slower than all the others. I yelled back at this soldier and directed him to get his "fat [behind] up and moving." At that moment the soldier raised his helmet and his "star" glistened in the California sunlight. It was General Pope.

Needless to say, I was sure that my goose would be cooked once we got to the top of the hill. However, this was not to be. General Pope approached me. I saluted him and he returned the salute. He then proceeded to tell me that I had performed admirably throughout the entire exercise. Not a word was said of my "unkind" remark to him. I learned later that General Pope had simply wanted to be part of the "exercise," and had "fallen in" with the platoon just as we had begun our "attack" on one of San Luis Obispo's infamous hills. Although the General and I met no more than a couple of times thereafter, he always impressed me by recognizing me as "the lieutenant on the hill."

Dave Herold reports: Upon arrival at Camp Old Gold in France, Co. L, 342 Inf. was assigned to guard duty for Division Headquarters. One cold, wet morning I was guarding the perimeter against the rumored presence of German paratroops, and as dawn was breaking I hid behind a large tree. This gave me a good view of the adjacent fields (and also offered some protection from the winds.) As the sun made its appearance, so did the occupant of the tent nearby. He immediately looked for the sentry, and when he saw me behind the tree he nodded and I nodded in return. As the sun rose and the danger lessened, I approached his tent. He finished shaving and asked me why I was hiding behind the tree. I explained: "If there were any Germans out there, I wanted to get the first shot." He laughed, and said he agreed with that. He then asked me where I was from, what was I going to do after the war, and seemed genuinely interested in my thoughts. He related a story of being an instructor at the University of Illinois, and several other personal observations. During this exchange, I finally realized that my new-found friend was General George Pope, and he reminded me of my favorite uncle. We parted. I continued my vigilance, and he rushed off to some meeting.

Robert Rasmus, Co. L, 342 Inf. reports:

Bob contributes words from Leo Kessler's *The Battle of the Ruhr Pocket* "after the 86th first day of attacking he [General Matthew Ridgeway] summoned [Gen. Melasky to his CP and told him his division's performance was "thoroughly unsatisfactory." [Melasky] tried to shift the blame to his assistant, George van Wyck Pope, and demanded that Pope should be relieved of his command." Ridgway agreed, and so did his boss, Gen. Hodges, but the Big Boss—Gen. Omar Bradley—stood up for Pope, and said he needed more time to prove himself. And so Pope stayed in the 86th Division.

General Omar Bradley says in his book, *A Soldier's Story*, "I had known Pope for years as a competent, amiable, and well-rounded soldier. He had been an instructor in my weapons section at Benning where I valued him as one of our best-qualified doughboys."

Richard Briggs, Co. I, 342 Inf., Division historian reports:

It was after Ridgeway ordered Melasky to be more aggressive, that the order was given to attack Ludenscheid, the largest city in the line of advance in the Ruhr Pocket. Gen. Pope immediately began to organize a Task Force. In the attack on Ludenscheid, I remember both Co. K and Co. L attacking up the main road from Attendorn to Ludenscheid. Just before we were to enter Ludenscheid, Co. I was to advance along a ridge that led directly into the city. While advancing, we became the target of a heavy artillery barrage. There were numerous deep bomb craters along the ridge and so I dove into one. Immediately someone landed on top of me. I thought it was one of my buddies. After a few long moments, the artillery let up, and we untangled and started to climb out. I remember him saying "It seems to be over, son." I looked up and saw a shiny star on his collar. I was amazed that it was Gen. Pope himself.

Richard gives additional details on Task Force Pope, both I and II, in his book "Blackhawks Over The Danube." Richard, Bob Rasmus, and Dave, along with the rest of the 3rd Battalion and Anti-Tank Co, 342 Inf, and 332 F A, Recon Troop, and 311 Engineers made up the Task Force.

The Best Pea Soup Ever
by Richard A. Phillips, 342nd B Co

It was one of those days in Germany when I pulled the duty of taking prisoners to the rear. Afterwards, two comrades and I hitched a ride back to find our company.

As we were coming into the next town, suddenly there was sniper fire. We jumped off the truck and headed for the nearest big house. While looking in vain for the sniper, dusk had descended. My comrades decided to search for Company B, but I opted to stay for the night and look in the morning.

The safest place was in the basement, and I soon learned that I had been preceded there by about 15 newly-released Polish slave laborers. We tried to communicate with each other—I knew no Polish, so I tried some feeble high school French. One guy knew a little French, but none of that worked very well.

I did understand that they were asking me if I had any food. I couldn't possibly feed them all with my two K rations, so I said "no." Some time later, I could see that several of them were busy cooking something in a pot. When they were done, they offered to share their meal with me. It turned out to be the best pea soup I have ever in my life tasted.

Blackhawk Twins I
by Hollis D. Duke 343rd D Co.

The Duke Twins

I grew up with my twin brother, Wallace Duke, in northeast Texas. We joined different units of the Army at different times, but that changed when Congress passed a law that permitted brothers to serve in the same unit: K Co. of the 343rd Infantry Regiment. The assignment may have been influenced by a letter our mother wrote to our Congressman, which was frowned on by our company commander. Soon after my arrival, I was summoned to appear before my new boss, who asked me to give up my corporal stripes and start over as a buck private. "I'll watch you and if you so much as stub your toe you will become a private anyway," he said. And watch me he did.

Serving together in the same unit had both good and bad points. It was good to be able to discuss home town gossip together, but I didn't enjoy it when Wallace would drive by in his Jeep during a march when I had sweat running off the tip of my nose and toot his little horn. "Hello George," he would say with a smile. (For no particular reason, we got in the habit of calling each other "George.")

In combat we had our separate missions, but I was always worried about that jeep-driving brother of mine. One morning I saw a jeep that was blown to bits. There was no body to be seen, but there was blood everywhere. Was it George or some other poor soul? Then there was the time when I went into a seaside village with friends on R and R and word went out that a GI had drowned in the surf. "George" never learned who it was, but he sure got upset with me because I had gone into the village to soak up some local culture. I guess he was watching out for me, too.

Blackhawk Twins II

Joseph Howard ("Howdy") and Henry ("Hank") Steers were born twenty minutes apart on a ranch in Dufur, Oregon, in 1922. Before they were a year old, the family moved to The Dalles, Oregon, where the "boys," as their grandmother called them, would spend the rest of their lives except for college at the University of Oregon and service as officers in the 86th Blackhawk Division in WW II. Howard led Co. 'L' weapons platoon and Henry was platoon leader of 'A' Co.. While in Germany, Hank was shot by an enemy sniper, which produced the story of "Hank's Helmet," related by his twin:

"… as we were crossing a valley, Hank was leading his platoon when suddenly he was knocked flat to the ground, stunned but conscious. He immediately got up and yelled to his messenger, 'What the hell happened?' There was a bullet hole through the helmet and the helmet liner as well. Good thing he had toilet paper in the top of the liner that was torn like confetti. Hank wore the helmet the rest of the war, thinking it a good luck charm. Even though the helmet no longer served as a useful wash basin, it served to prevent any more "close ones."

After military service, the twins returned to college where they graduated with Bachelor of Science degrees in science and physical education. There followed teaching careers which made them first-name friends of everyone in town, and continued involvement in sports: pool games at the Elks Lodge and golf four or five times a week, weather permitting. When Howard died in 2001, Henry had to be taken to a nursing home. As they were wheeling him out of the transport, Henry was seen clutching his "good omen," his Blackhawk helmet.

Information for the story of the Steers twins was graciously supplied by their cousin, Theodore R. Spinning, a career member of the U.S. Marine Corps. Semper Fi, Ted.

A Long and Winding Road
by Thomas Kelsey

It was a long and winding road that my father, Charles Kelsey (86th Division's 911th Field Artillery Battalion, Battery B) followed to get his Purple Heart medal 53 years after WWII ended.

In 1945 Pvt. Charles Kelsey was a gunner on a 105 mm Howitzer in Germany just weeks before the Nazis surrendered to Allied forces. In early April, his convoy moved out from Hagen in the Ruhr Pocket headed for Plattenburg, but he never got there. Sniper fire hit the truck in which he was riding, which caused the howitzer it was pulling to overturn into a ditch. Kelsey was crushed under artillery shells and the cannon, and was left paralyzed in a field hospital for three weeks.

Lost or misplaced records resulted in him returning home without his Purple Heart. He was turned down twice before Sen. John McCain intervened on his behalf to get the ball rolling in 1996. Letters were written on his behalf by several of his Blackhawk comrades, a doctor who treated him in Germany, and his commanding officer, Maj. Paul Foster living in Colorado.

When he learned in 1998 that he would get his medal, Dad said "I broke down after waiting 53 years." The Purple Heart was presented to him by Congresswoman Loretta Sanchez. When he and my mother, Madalyn, started to attend Blackhawk Association reunions in the 80's many of the men he had served with thought he had died during the war.

My daughter Sierra, who was 12 when my dad got his medal, asked me what the medal meant. I replied: "You should be really proud of your Grandpa. He was wounded fighting for our country. He was doing his job."

A Day in The Ruhr Remembered
by Robert M. Coulbourn III 343rd I Co.

At 0430 Hours on April 12, 1945 we began our approach march toward Altendorn in the Ruhr Pocket. After marching several hours and passing the town we came to an open hillside with a town on top. A German in a house ahead of us fired on us and our machine gunners returned fire. S/Sgt "Bud" Tordorff suffered a compound fracture of his thigh at this time. Multi-barrelled 20mm anti-aircraft guns sprayed the hills and the woods where we were and two riflemen were wounded. There was intermittent sniper fire, some very close to our heads. Our mortar section fired on suspected Wehrmacht positions.

After this action ceased, a column of about 1,000 Germans, seemingly civilians, came from the village toward us. Then the company advanced to the town, secured it and stopped there for an hour. At about 1100 Hours we marched down the opposite side of the hill into a valley where we engaged the enemy again.... After some maneuvering, I Co. entered the town and later we marched through it. At approximately 1800, as we started to leave the town by a road through a deep draw, 88's opened up on us. We changed our route and started up a narrow dirt road. As our leading platoon reached four houses beside the road, we were fired on once again by automatic weapons, including 20 mm guns in the hills ahead of us. There was practically no cover; some men sought protection in a water-filled ditch; the rest of us just hugged the slight rise beside the road. Several men in the leading platoon were wounded. A few minutes after being fired on, Harvey had us set up our mortars. Our gun was the first in action and we covered the fence line 800 yards ahead of us and the hillside to the right. Heavy machine guns behind us sprayed the hillside.

At about 2000 Hours the Germans had withdrawn and our dwindling supply of ammunition had been replenished. The company reorganized and spent the night in four houses beside the road. The four tank destroyers attached to the company had followed us all day and had not done any good. That night security patrols were sent out.

It was just another day in World War II.

I Remember Al Joslyn, Private for Life
by Austin Goodrich, 342nd K Co.

Al topped out rank-wise as a private. He couldn't read or claimed he couldn't, and I used to write his letters to his mom to whom he sent his pay and substantial poker winnings. Al was not only skilled in playing cards, he was the luckiest card player I've ever known. He'd draw to an inside straight and against all odds fill it nine times out of ten.

But what I most clearly remember about Al was the way he mocked prescribed military courtesy without a single trace of disrespect. Whenever he spotted Maj. Ward, at whatever distance, he shouted, "Hi, Big Boy!" And our battalion commander without fail cupped his hands to his mouth and shouted back, "Hi, Al." In similar fashion, Al always load-mouthedly addressed our Battalion Exec, Captain Mocker, as "Shorty." And Capt. Mocker always responded with a huge smile and a "How ya doin' Al?" These fine officers won my undying admiration and respect for putting human compassion above all conventions, including military rules of addressing superior officers.

The only officer I can recall who bullied or pulled rank on Al Joslyn was a mean little lieutenant. This "90-day wonder" (our title for fast-course officers' training school graduates) was loudly booed by enlisted personnel when he deliberately made a dirty hook slide into Al in a softball game and laughed at his writhing victim.

Al wasn't exactly a hero. He was wounded during combat in the Ruhr Valley, but not by enemy action. He got his purple heart after a half-track hit against his leg when Al got too close picking up a cigar tossed out by the armored troops. After the war, Al wasn't smart enough to file a medical claim at the separation center, but later I got together with him in our home town of Battle Creek, MI. He walked with a bad limp, and I asked my Dad, an Attorney, if he could get some sort of compensation for Al, who came from a poor family on the other side of the tracks in Hunkytown, where most of my football teammates lived. Against all odds, he established "service connection" and lifetime VA compensation for Al's disability. My love for my father hit a new high and remained there.

Apple Ass Vogel, M.D.
by Chuck Bernstein, 343rd L Co

Little has been written about the often-heroic exploits of the medics in wartime. The medics: aid men, doctors, surgeons, nurses and ambulance/hearse drivers are virtually overlooked in the reports of the life and death struggles of WWII combat in Europe. Only a smattering is known, mostly comedic, of their role in the Pacific as seen in the TV sitcom *MASH*, set during the Korean War.

In the ETO the medics' bravery was commonplace. Zigzagging full tilt between falling bombs, deadly machinegun and sniper fire and tiptoeing fearlessly as if on a high wire through deadly minefields, medics would locate, treat and rescue the wounded G.I.. If hit, we were taught to call out "medic!," which would bring a medic, undaunted by shot and shell, to assist us.

Our chief medic in the Third Battalion of the 343rd was a somewhat disheveled, rumpled, devil-may-care Army Captain M.D., who rarely wore a tie or bothered to shine or even to lace up his shoes. Every "grunt" in our unit had a nickname, and because the first name on our doctor's nameplate simply read "A.A." and because on rising from his office chair the most prominent part of him was his rotund rear end, we gleefully christened him *Apple Ass*.

A GI with a physical problem never needed an appointment to see Apple-Ass but simply joined the long line that snaked around his office during Sick Call. The group always included a few shirkers we called "gold bricks," trying to squirm out of joining in the day's exhausting hike and/or brutal firefight. It seemed Apple-Ass could recognize these men by intuition. Though he carefully examined and patiently listened to all complaints, many of which should have been brought to the Chaplain, he did what he could for the truly sick and wounded before, if necessary, hurriedly sending them on to the nearest field hospital.

When you entered his cramped combination infirmary-office-lab-pharmacy-treatment room and hospital, you'd usually find AA comfortably seated on a reclining chair behind his worn oak desk looking like the wise old owl he was. at we didn't know about him was that after each battle ole Apple Ass would insist on riding out with his medical crew to the field of carnage. Pulling on paper-thin gloves, he'd scrupulously comb through the area, salvaging dog tags, bloody pieces of arms, legs, finger, toes, earlobes and eyeballs that by some medical magic might be replaced or reattached to bodies of the wounded who had been earlier removed.

More disturbing was the information leaked by his medical staff that in civilian life he'd lost both his wife and young son in a horrible car accident. That on returning with his staff from a battle site he'd lock himself in his office with a bottle of whiskey. From outside his door, his staff could hear prolonged, muffled sobbing. It was said that he'd recognized some lad or part of one, whom he'd recently treated and whom he'd reluctantly "returned to duty" as a body torn to shreds. He suffered the memory silently.

He was Army-by-the-book while quietly caring, guardedly concerned. He looked on us as *his children*, his guys. That was more important to him than whether his tie was properly knotted or his shoes were shined, or even laced. Ole Apple-Ass represents to me the Army's risk-taking, self-sacrificing mission of all our medics in WW II. Now standing at attention, with my hand over my heart, I salute them with my silent but profound thanks.

Blackhawk Duty, A Family Tradition
by James K. Logsdon

My father, Kellogg Logsdon, served with the 342nd Regiment of the 86th Infantry Division in WW I, the war in Europe that was supposed to end all wars. He enlisted the day after war was declared, and was first sent to Camp Grant near Rockford, Illinois, where he was accepted into Officers Training School. He told me that the Army training was the most demanding regime he ever experienced; frequently after a long day in the field he would bite his lip just to stay awake to study.

He excelled as an officer and was assigned as cadre to provide training for officer candidates. Eventually he sailed to England and from there to France for final pre-combat training with the 342nd Infantry Regiment. According to practice in those days, the troops were billeted in local homes, and Dad got to reside in the chateau of the Baroness du Cadillac. Among his happy experiences was ushering at the wedding of the Baroness's granddaughter. When the musicians struck up *Les Marseilles* Dad remarked to the Baroness that it was a wonderful anthem.

"Not for me," she replied, "My grandfather was guillotined as it was played. When the regiment marched to trains for the front, young girls ran beside the soldiers and pinned rosettes to their collars. This was a lasting joyful memory for Dad, who was engaged in a bridge game with the Colonel when news of the armistice was announced. Sadly, at a stop one of the soldiers stepped off the train and was killed by a train streaking in the opposite direction. "Stick the body in the luggage car," the colonel ordered. Dad thought what a very sad message that would be for a mother whose hopes would have been raised by the Armistice news.

My dad became a company commander and should have been made a captain, but when the war ended so did promotions and he remained a 1st Lieutenant. Employed in a brokerage firm after his discharge, Dad was asked if he could manage as many as 20 employees. Chuckling, he said since he had commanded 200 men in the army, this should be no problem.

James Kellogg Logsdon—served as Lieutenant, US Army, 1953–55. Grandson Craig Warner served as B-52 pilot in the US Air Force 1973–1980 and as Marine Corps Major C-130 pilot 1984–1990.

The 86th Blackhawk Division Memorial Highway

The 86th Blackhawk Memorial Highway—Thanks to Larry Bennett!

Several years of dedicated work by Association Secretary Larry Bennett resulted in the official dedication of a major New York highway to the 86th Blackhawk Division. Bennett made full use of his contacts with legislators of both parties in tirelessly pushing for the bill even after he left the Assembly in 1985. One of the sponsors, Republican Senator Bill Larkin praised our division as "a critical component of the United States Army," noting that "the heroic actions of these soldiers represents the tremendous sacrifices they made to defend, protect, and preserve the freedoms we cherish. Naming this portion of the New York State Highway system after them is just one small way of recognizing these special individuals and expressing the gratitude all New Yorkers feel for their sacrifice."

The bill adds a new section to the N.Y. Highway Law to designate Route 9W from the border of Orange & Rockland County north through all of Orange County and a portion of Ulster County terminating in the town of Esopus at the bridge that spans the Roundout Creek as the "86th Blackhawk Infantry Division Memorial Highway." Newspaper accounts noted that we were one of only a very few Army units to serve in both the European and Pacific theaters in WW II.

REUNION GUEST SPEAKER: SOLDIER BOB DOLE
by Dick Behrends 331st FA

"Bob" Dole – Reunion guest speaker

We were pleased and honored to have a very special comrade in arms, Bob Dole, speak to us at our reunion banquet on September 9, 2006. After a lifetime in public service, including 27 years as a U.S. Senator and presidential candidate in 1966, Bob Dole credits his nearly fatal combat experience for teaching him patience and adaptability. "Patience is an acquired trait," he has written, "and I've spent a lifetime patiently trying to acquire it. Most of us want patience and we want it now. But few things will cause you to stop and focus on the moment, as well as on the big picture, more than not being able to feed yourself for more than a year."

In his memoir titled simply *One Soldier's Story*, Bob Dole discounts the claim of ours being *the greatest generation*. "Truth be told," he writes, "we were ordinary Americans fated to confront extraordinary tests. Every generation of young men and women who dare to face the realities of war—fighting for freedom, defending our country, with a willingness to lay their lives on the line—is the greatest generation."

After performing dozens of operations on Bob Dole, his surgeon, Hampar Kelikan, was often asked why he didn't just give it up. "Because," he would respond, "This young man had the faith to endure." "To me, writes Dole, "that comment was one of the greatest honors I've ever received." It was a high honor for us to have Bob Dole speak at our reunion.

How We Almost Destroyed The Sound of Music
by Francis J. "Noot" Landry, 86th Signal Co.

May 5, 1945—Victory in Europe Day—found elements of the 86th Blackhawk Division's Signal Co. in Oberndorf, Austria. This picture post card village at the base of the beautiful snow-capped Alps was where "Silent Night" was composed. It was also near the place where some other wonderful music was composed.

German soldiers emerged from the woods with hands upraised just like in the movies. I remember how young they looked, like teenagers, tired, hungry and scared. We had been warned, however, that there could be some fanatics among them so "be alert." Early the next morning as I rounded a building I saw figures emerging from the mist in the distance. The sun was directly behind them and the lead figure seemed to be carrying a machine gun. I called out to my friend Bob Webb "Grab your rifle, Bob, someone's approaching and they're armed." As we took up positions and were about to open up on them, I shouted "hold your fire, I hear something." It was the sound of music coming down from the mountain sung, it seemed to me, by the Baron von Trapp children fleeing from the Nazis. I have often been haunted by the thought of how close we came to firing on those children and denying future generations their wonderful music.

Random Blackhawk Musings
by Austin Goodrich, 342nd K Co.

I now have two grandsons in the service, one in the Army, one in the Marine Corps. Talking with them I am struck by how similar military life is today compared with when I served more than half a century ago. Perhaps the most noticeable difference is the large number of women who now serve in the infantry, which used to be for men only. Come to think of it, why shouldn't both men and women serve together in infantry units? I seem to recall that we spent most of our time standing around waiting for someone to tell us where to go and what to do when we got there. Why, it was really very much like being married.

Although the 86th Division was organized like any other infantry division, its personnel differed in one important respect. At its lowest level were boys with IQs above 120 who had been headed for college in the ASTP program or were about to join the Air Force as cadets. The non-commissioned officer command levels were staffed with older men most of whom hadn't got beyond sixth grade. Their IQ's will not be recorded here.

It was Plato's *Utopia* turned upside down, with the smartest and best educated at the bottom of the ladder and the less educated men at the top. A recipe for disaster? One would certainly think so. But strangely enough, it worked. The schoolroom smarts at the bottom somehow blended with the street smarts of those in command to produce an effective fighting force, a combat infantry unit which won the praise of all of the generals who led it, including Omar Bradley and George Patton.

Like all of my buddies, I'm proud to say that I was an infantryman—one of the thirty percent of soldiers in the US Army who suffered seventy percent of total casualties in World War II. Some of those casualties were accidental, but nonetheless final. Some of them haunt my memory more than sixty years after they happened.

I recall with chilling clarity what happened one day when we were preparing to move up to the front on the Rhine River outside the cathedral city of Cologne. We'd just been issued live ammunition and were busy cleaning our weapons. My assistant light machine-gunner, Steve Jarvis, had just finished cleaning his sub-machine gun, the so-called "grease gun, a .45 caliber weapon that was both easy to operate and cost only nine dollars and 99 cents to manufacture. Well, you get what you pay for. You could never hit your target with the M-3 unless you were aiming at the sky, because the gun rose up quickly when fired. There was another problem with this bargain basement weapon. After cleaning it, there was only one way to move the bolt forward and that was to pull the trigger. If there happened to be a loaded magazine in place when you did this, the weapon fired. That's how Steve accidentally shot poor Joe Vittrano, ammo bearer, who was seated just a few feet away. Joe would have been killed but for a pocket Bible he carried in his shirt pocket. The lethal .45 caliber bullet bounced off Joe's bible and ricocheted down and out of his arm. We all assumed that if Joe survived, he would be sewn up and given a medical discharge. No such luck. A few guys ran into him about eight months later in the Philippines, but the man who accidentally shot him never saw him again.

I exchanged letters with Steve a few years ago and asked if he had ever been able to get in touch with Joe after the war. He wrote that he had not been able to locate his accidental victim, but that the incident continued to produce terrible fits of depression and nightmares.

* * * * * * *

The hand grenade was another weapon that could kill friend and foe alike. We had just been issued grenades—four to a customer—as we prepared to move into battle in a mountain town in the Ruhr. Somehow we heard that the cool thing to do was to straighten the ends of the ring wire that held the handle in place and prevented the grenade from exploding prematurely. Everyone did this. Unfortunately a rifleman in the first platoon loosened the mechanism a little too much before attaching the grenade to his back pack. When he shifted his weight as he relaxed outside the village church, the pin fell out and the grenade hissed into life before ending the life of Pfc Muldoon exactly four and a half seconds later. I buried my grenades in my fox hole when we pulled out of town.

* * * * * * * * *

Then there was the day in mid March 1945 when we came under the so-called "friendly fire" of our own artillery. We had marched all day and were taking a break in a pine forest above the church town of Hilchenbach in preparation for our first night attack. Artillery shells were heard lazily crossing overhead as the bombardment began to soften resistance to our scheduled attack. No one paid any attention. We'd only been in combat for a couple of weeks, but we knew that the shell you could hear wouldn't hurt you, didn't have your name on it. Word was passed "not to worry," it's our own. What was a bit troubling was that the shells were getting lower in the sky, closer to the tall evergreens rising above us. Then it happened: six or eight or maybe a dozen shells exploded right over our heads. All hell broke loose. I think tree-hugging was invented that night. The ground was too hard to dig in so I tried to save my ass by becoming a part of a tall pine tree. And I prayed for God to make 'em stop.

Then very suddenly a terrible silence wrapped in a sour-sweet cloud of cordite descended on our hillside. Through the calls for "Medic, medic, over here, medic," I heard a call that continues to haunt my memory. Heard it only once. It was Pfc Marks, a rifleman in the 3rd platoon, a practical joker whose face was always smiling, as if he'd just pulled off a successful practical joke. Marks had called out one word: "Mother." To hear the end of this story, you'll have to buy a copy of my memoirs. (BORN TO SPY).

That night we moved into the town of Hilchenbach, which was occupied by the battle-hardened troops of the Panzer Lehr Division. The next morning, a detail of "volunteers" from my platoon was sent back into the woods to retrieve the men who had been wounded and killed there the night before. They were all captured and held prisoners for a day or two by German troops. One member of this detail was John List. It was John List, who 25 years after the war took a war souvenir pistol in hand and shot and killed his mother, his wife and their three teen-aged children. After living under an assumed name in Colorado for about 20 years, John was captured as the result of his appearance on the America's Most Wanted TV show.

An interesting sidelight on the life of my platoon mate John List is this: He was officially diagnosed as suffering from post traumatic stress disorder for which he received treatment and 10 percent disability compensation from the Veterans Administration. Could this medical condition explain why John List, by far the most gentle person I have ever known, became a family murderer? This question was addressed by the judge who passed judgment on John. He claimed that List's army combat was an irrelevant issue, because when he was questioned by a psychiatrist, John could not remember any details of his combat experience. The sad fact is that the blocking out of traumatic experiences is a hallmark symptom of post traumatic stress disorder.

Are John List and his murdered family members to be viewed as victims of this disorder—the collateral damage of war? I do think so.

* * * * * * *

Back to the subject of fighting in the Ruhr pocket. There was humor as well as tragedy. During a fierce fire fight in the city of Ludenscheid, right in the middle of the city square, an apartment house door was suddenly thrown open and a German business man emerged. With his umbrella raised on high and his briefcase on top of his head, the man shouted "sivilist" (civilian) and jogged across the street explaining that it was necessary for him to get to his office, so could we please stop all the shooting there on his street, the hauptstrasse of Ludenscheid.

Another bittersweet memory of mine stems from a small bungalow where we were earlier billeted on the outskirts of Cologne. As I lay on a small bed trying to get some sleep my eyes were drawn to a needlepoint wall hanging. It read

Ich bin klein, mein hertz mach rein;
Soll nieman dritt wohnen als Jesu allein.

Which translates to;

"I am small, make my heart clean, So no one will live there but Jesus alone."

My mother had taught me this prayer when I was a little kid. My God!

The absolute madness of war made a chill run through my body. Here I was in Germany, the homeland of my father's family, reading a child's prayer I had learned as a kid from my Mom. Here I was about to move across the Rhine River and kill as many of my distant relatives as possible. Crazy? Yes. There's no other word for it.

* * * * * * *

Actually I didn't kill nearly as many Germans as I took prisoner. Most of the Wehrmacht knew they were beaten by the time we arrived and were only to happy to surrender to the Americans. The Red Army on the eastern front didn't take many prisoners.

One evening I was on guard duty at a fenced enclosure that contained several thousand German prisoners of war, when I heard a small voice from the other side of the barbed wire.

"Excuse me. Mister. Psst, I'm down here."

I looked through the wire to see a baby-faced kid in a gray German uniform.

"Whatcha want?" I asked. We weren't supposed to talk with prisoners.

"I, uh. I'm an American."

"The hell you say. What are you doing in a German uniform?"

"Well, see, years go, I came over here with my parents to visit family in Hungary. Then the war started and we couldn't leave to go home to America."

I looked down to see tears in the eyes of this kid, who had been drafted into a Wehrmacht Labor Battalion.

"I'll see what I can do," I said, and gave him a chocolate bar from my K ration.

* * * * * * *

After the Ruhr, we joined Patton's Third Army and raced southeast all the way to the Danube River. We hated ol' Blood and Guts. He moved so fast, we never got any sleep, never had a decent meal, never got to take a shower. And we never got any clean clothes. (I went through a month of combat wearing some German civilian's black pants after mine were shredded getting through a barbed wire fence.) Only years later did I realize that I owed my life to Gen Patton, who moved so fast that the enemy never knew where we were coming from. Finally, deep in Bavaria we did encounter some heavy resistance mainly from diehard members of the SS and the grounded Luftwaffe. Not to mention the dreaded anti-tank, anti-aircraft artillery weapons, the eighty-eights (88 millimeter caliber.) These canons had the muzzle velocity of rifles, which produced a blood-chilling effect when they screamed over your head. In an effort to avoid them, I had found refuge in an abandoned German fox hole in Ingolstadt on the banks of the Danube. Suddenly something metallic bounced off my helmet and I thought I'd bought the farm. As it turned out, the object was a .50 calibre shell casing that had fallen from an American fighter plane strafing a farm shed that might have been an enemy observation post across the river.

At sundown, just when we had hopes of getting a night's sleep in a nearby apartment house, the order came down that we were to cross the Danube river. We were told that General Patton himself had issued the order. As if that would make it any more popular with us. Under heavy enemy mortar fire, we dragged wooden skiffs down to the river bank, jumped in and paddled for all we were worth. When we reached the other shore I jumped out and helped my squad leader, who didn't know how to swim, to get out on dry land. At the same time I had to hold on to the boat in a terribly swift current. Since I only had two hands, something had to go. My machine gun disappeared in the muddy waters. After another guy got hold of a tree on the river bank, I dove into the icy waters of that not-so-blue Danube to retrieve my gun.

And I want to tell you, that sitting in a foxhole that night, soaking wet, was not the most pleasant experience I've ever had. But it was by far the coldest one. That night was even more unpleasant for the troops who were drowned in the river, and there were many. At one point a G.I. I recognized by his voice as the Captain of L Company came stumbling along the river bank asking in a loud whisper if we had seen anyone from "L" Company. We hadn't. The company commander couldn't locate a single one of the hundred plus members of his command. Now, that's what's called "missing in action."

* * * * * * *

A week later, after crossing the Isar River and the Isar Mittel canal, we had a fierce encounter with some tough German troops in the town of Berglern. Years later, our entire company was awarded Bronze Stars for that action. I had used up all of my ammunition when the call came for me to provide covering fire so that our medic could reach our beloved company commander, Captain Macalester, who lay wounded in a field. And I was out of ammunition. Captain Mac, who preferred marching straight ahead under enemy fire instead of taking cover—a tactic known as marching fire—died trying to end the war as soon as possible, and to this day I blame myself for not being able to help save him. There's a whole bunch of guilt in war.

Recollections of War
by Abraham Rutman, 311 Medics C Co.

To generals huddled over maps studded with multi-colored pins and flags to display troop deployments with circles and arrows, WWII appears to be neat and orderly. To rank and file members of an infantry division the view is quite different, blurred by tragic-comic tears that appear six decades later.

As A Jew living in Montreal, I enlisted in the Canadian Army to join in the fight against Hitler who was killing Jews. Canada was even less prepared than the U.S., training with broomsticks for rifles, so the two allies agreed to let Canadians serve in the U.S. Army. On to Camp Livingston, where I learned to trap pigs for roasts and to keep warm in the winter by putting a puppy dog at the bottom of my sleeping bag. Thence to Californina where we were taught to jump off landing craft at first onto a sandy beach, then in three feet of water and finally into a pounding ten-foot surf.

Linguistically, I could communicate with friend and foe alike in Europe. My Yiddish helped me speak with Germans and my Montreal French enabled me to speak with the people of Normandy where we were first billeted in tent camps named after cigarette brands. There we could swap a 5-cent pack of cigarettes for a bottle of 120 proof homebrewed Calvados.

With General Patton's 3rd Army I remember how we took refuge in the dark basement of a small bungalow only to discover that we shared space with two Wehrmacht soldiers. We agreed that if their side succeeded in a counter-attack, we'd become their prisoners or vice versa. Not all German troops were this congenial. We discovered Waffen SS (Hitler's elite troops) who had broken fingers of captured G.I.'s in truck doors before they stacked them like firewood, doused them with gasoline and incinerated them. After that we showed no mercy to SS troops.

We witnessed another form of atrocity when we liberated a slave labor camp where under a sign that proclaimed *Arbeit Macht Frei* (Labor Liberates), we were greeted by starving women who were unable to breast feed an emaciated infant. Some of these half-dead women were reduced to eating grass in the meadow like grazing cattle.

At the Isar river, an officer selected ten "volunteers," who were given six paddles to cross the fast-moving river in a wooden skiff. On the far bank a Kraut soldier was shot and fell backwards. Had he fallen forward, he would have detonated explosives that would have blown many of us sky high.

Then it ended, and we were welcomed into New York harbor by bathing beauties dancing on a barge. As these floating stages circled around our ships, we moved from side to side for a better view, which nearly caused the ship to capsize, but we couldn't care less. We were home and the war was nearly over. Thank God!

Combat: Up close and Personal
by Logan E. (Larry) Calhoun, 341 L Co.

Note: *In the perception of the top brass at Supreme Headquarters, Hagen was a city in the Ruhr Valley where units of the 75th and 86th divisions met to split in two the industrial heartland of the third Reich. As seen by 86th Division infantrymen who had fought through some of the most inhospitable terrain in the European Theatre to reach it, Hagen was just another day of combat.*

Artillery rounds were falling within the block as we entered Hagen. We had been told that our way was clear which wasn't the case at all. The Germans were on top of a hill with a cemetery and had lowered their 88's to use as artillery along with one or more machine guns. Platoon Leader Lt. Earle Buck was severely wounded, as were many others. Platoon Sgt. Frank Harris, Pfcs. Phillip See, Howard Pringle and Nicholas Chan, were all killed within the half hour.

While I was pinned down by the 88's and machinegun fire, Pfc. Orie Coil, 2nd Platoon, a few inches in front of me was hit several times in the leg and foot. Each time he was hit his blood splattered my glasses. (Later on hospital leave, Coil visited us at Camp Crowder and his leg was so drawn that his heel wouldn't touch the floor.)

As the First Platoon led by Lt. Pennington was flanking the Germans, I worked my way up into the cemetery. Company Commander Bobby Smith called and told me to stay with him, which I did for the rest of the war. We passed a shell hole and looking down saw one of our medics, T/3 Paul Pyeritz trying to bandage one of our wounded. I told Capt. Smith "The medic is wounded worse than the guy he is trying to bandage. He should get a medal." (He was awarded the Silver Star. Other comrades who received the Silver Star were TSgt Frank Harris, Lt. Earle Buck and Lt. Henry Pennington.)

Co. L casualties in that day's action: 6KIA, 30WIA.

Collateral Damage
by John List 342nd K Co.

After we got back to the States, I often wondered why we were sent to Europe, since we didn't get into any real fighting. [!] For the same reason I couldn't understand why we had all been awarded the Combat Infantry Badge. Years later, after I'd read *Blackhawks Over the Danube* (by Richard Briggs) which recounts all of the action that K Company was in, I realized that we had engaged in our fair share of combat. My squad leader, Joe Heitman, documented in detail some of the fighting that we had. Joe mentioned that in the fighting at Berglern, for which we were later awarded the Bronze Star, our mortar squad fired all of its 40 rounds. Joe also remembered how he had fired his M-1 carbine until he had run out of ammo. To this day I don't remember those actions, or that my assistant gunner, "Doc" Iverson, had dropped a single shell into the tube of my 60 mm mortar. Perhaps my old friend, Patrick H. Daoust, MD, shed some clinical light on my condition in a letter to me dated August 10, 1997:

"David Herold's Log [342-L] mentions a day that sounds very much like the day you said you could remember only the beginning and the end of during which you were told you fired over 40 mortar rounds to break up a German attack at [Berglern] It sounds to me like a clear-cut case of amnesia. This kind of amnesia would only result from extreme mental trauma. In your case it would occur in a person who was basically very strong but who at the same time possessed a very gentle nature. Thus, your actions on that day would have run very counter to that gentle nature, which not surprisingly would produce amnesia. This would account for the fact that not only on that day, but at other times during your involvement in combat situations, you had no recollection of your experiences. Your memory of these situations simply produced a blank screen. I believe very strongly that it's highly likely that you did suffer from Post Traumatic Stress Disorder and that this very well could have influenced your subsequent behavior."

Ed Comment: John List was sentenced to five consecutive life terms for the murder of his mother, wife and three teen-aged children in 1971. After living under an alias for nearly 18 years in Colorado, John was captured as a result of a report by a former neighbor, who recognized him from a sculpture televised on the TV program, America's Most Wanted. List died in prison of natural causes in March 2008. John List's personal memoirs written with Austin Goodrich were published in 2006 by iUniverse (www.iuniverse.com).

The following comments were supplied by John List's Blackhawk buddies:

Squad leader Joe Heitman (deceased) Our entry into Austria marked the last day of the war. In retrospect, I wonder that anyone in K Co. got out alive ... At the very least, we should thank John for being a good soldier.

Bob Guernsey, Mortar Squad mate: I don't remember any notable events involving John. I thought he was a good soldier and friend. I don't understand the tragedy many years later that engulfed him and those connected to him. I feel sorry for John, but I feel sorrier for those who suffered because of him.

Lloyd "Doc" Iverson, Mortar Squad mate: The only thing I remember about John is that he was very much a loner, attended church quite faithfully, and I thought conscientious about his duties as a soldier.

Walt "Rusty" Hayes, Mortar Squad mate: I remember John as being quiet, meek, studious and the last person you'd ever expect violence from. I retain a mental image of him as tall and lanky, with glasses being a dominant feature along with an oversized helmet that always looked in danger of falling off.

Steve Jarvis, 4th Platoon mate: John and I were especially good friends in K Col, sharing a love of classical music, and generally being very compatible personalities. We spent many hours together in camp and in town, especially in St. Louis Obispo, CA, at the library and in the booths of music stores listening to classical music records. I think John and I were attracted to each other because we both had rather introverted personalities. We got along quite well, perhaps boring each other, but liking each other despite our absolutely opposing philosophical, religious and political views.

When John disappeared, I sincerely hoped he was a suicide. I can understand, in a manner of speaking, what life must have been like for him: a demented wife torturing him constantly, a very unsympathetic mother to his children, and as a result children who probably gave him no respect, and were no doubt rebellious. Yet his sense of duty to his family and his religious beliefs precluded his running away or committing suicide, which I would probably have done. Instead, he had an emotional breakdown which must have turned him into another person. There's no doubt about the extensive premeditation in the crime, which does not at all square with the John of before or since.

Paul Mallon K Company comrade: I thought John to be highly intelligent but rather introverted and when after the war I heard that he had become an accountant, I thought it an appropriate niche for his type of personality. I find it hard to believe, however, that he could remember no combat situations in Germany. Ours was certainly not a "D Day" epic, but there were situations both in the Ruhr and afterwards when we were under hostile fire and taking casualties and I, for one, felt it very much a real war.

My post-war contacts with John occurred in the mid-60's when he accepted a position with a Jersey City bank as comptroller and we got together periodically for luncheon and gossip. Towards the end of the [60's] decade (when he was selling life insurance) he seemed in good spirits and happy. I had several more meetings with him and learned that he was experiencing difficulties in sales and feeling financial pressures. The news of his rampage in late 1971 came like a bombshell and I found it hard to believe. He did not seem the type and I became convinced that he must have experienced some sort of mental breakdown.

Austin "Red" Goodrich, Platoon mate: John List came across as the most gentle soul I had ever known. He smiled a lot, was soft-spoken, never swore or told dirty jokes and was kind to everyone. He was built like a pear and always appeared to be on the verge of tripping over his own feet. All of which made one feel a little sorry for this church-going scholar being immersed in the dirty-minded, rough and tumble life of the infantry. He just didn't fit in the Army mold. Only later did I come to admire his intellect and feel compassion for his tragic inability to cope with the harsh realities of an ungentle world.

PART THREE

FINALE

Philippine Islands: September 1945 to April 1946 Back to US, discharge and return to civilian life.

Frank Burns: An Early Blackhawk Businessman

Filthy Frank Sets Up Shop in the Philippines

Few Reunion attendees may realize that our Association 1st Vice President, Frank Burns, also served for many years as the Program Director responsible for putting together the reunion program. It's a huge job, but nothing's too big for the Blackhawk who got into business as the founder and president of Filthy Frank's Laundry in the Philippine Islands in 1945. Frank learned then that if you could identify a need and provide a service to satisfy it at a reasonable price, you'd make a profit and a lot of friends.

The need was for a laundry to wash and iron GI fatigues and khakis, which in the heat and humidity of the Philippines became malodorous after 24 hours, at a reasonable price. Philippine women working on river banks charged $2 for a set of khakis. Frank bought used washing machines and some used hand irons, fashioned name tags out of some scrap aluminum and went into business. For a charge of 50 cents a month, every member of the 341st Service Co. got their clothes cleaned. When Frank left for home in February 1946, his business was still going strong. And Frank put in the next 31 years helping Minnesota Mining and Manufacturing become a giant in the business world! Now he's the main man behind our great reunion programs.

A Star was Born … in Manila 1945

Joe Garagiola, Star Player and Broadcaster

Blackhawk baseball fans will recognize the young man who moved from the baseball diamond in Manila, P.I. where he played for an all star team of 86th Div dogfaces, to the National League's St. Louis Cardinals. Yes, it's Joe Garagiola, who retired in Phoenix, AZ after a great baseball career. The all-star catcher, who later worked as baseball broadcaster, TV personality, dog show m.c. and author (Baseball Is A Funny Game) responded to our Bugle request for his recollection of the days when he played with other Major League stars Kirby Higbe (Dodgers), who earned more from a Dodgers retainer fee than the Division's Commanding General earned in a year. Also on the team was Hall of Fame pitcher Early Wynn of the Cleveland Indians, whose intimidating bean ball was so feared that Higbe kept him off the mound and hadt him play second base on the Blackhaw team.

"You really challenge me to think of something that happened so long ago," Joe wrote to the Bugle. "I do remember that Kirby Higbe was our manager and that he had only 2 signals: you always had the green light to hit regardless of the count, and if Higbe was on first, don't ever try to get to third, because he'd be standing there. I never had another manager who came close to those two signs."

Joe's son, Joe Garagiola, Jr., served as general manager of the Arizona Diamond Backs before moving into the baseball commissioner's office.

One Down, One to Go

In an interview published in the Greensboro (NC) News Record, Association President Dick Behrends recalled some postwar duty in the Philippines.

We had trucks to transport Japanese prisoners to a holding facility. By the time we had them loaded, there was only room for them to stand up, packed shoulder to shoulder. We had about a three-hour trip to get back to the division compound and had to go through a number of small villages where the grass huts lined the narrow roads. When our column drove through villages, the Philippine civilians dumped their garbage, and anything else they could find on top of the prisoners. Some even threw rocks and other heavy objects that seriously hurt the Japanese.

The prisoners were all pretty emaciated after hiding out in the jungle with very little food. The trip was difficult for them, but when we arrived at their internment destination and washed off all the debris, they were relieved to still be alive, with food to eat, clean water to drink and ultimately a trip back home.

After seven months in the Philippines, we got the news that we were going home to be discharged in April, 1946. We were the first full division to get back to the U.S. from Europe and one of only two divisions to serve in both the European and Pacific theaters. Newspapers from coast to coast ran stories on our return home. The front page of the Chicago Tribune published a photo of me shaving a fellow Blackhawk with a captured German sword.

A Good People Loyal and Industrious
by Duncan McHolm, 343rd AT Co.

At our camp in Marakina I received my toughest assignment outside of actual combat—Division Labor Officer. Our mission was to round up Jap stragglers and to rehabilitate the people. With the help of Thomas Banatin, a local hero who had led guerrilla warfare against the Japanese occupiers, we hired almost a thousand workers in the area. They were graded as Master Carpenter, Carpenter and laborers. They had to be paid at the end of each week, and the Division Finance Officer had told me he wanted no re-lining; i.e., get everybody paid ever week. I had a well-educated Filipino college graduate who made this possible.

I established a Pay Station of wire mesh in a corner of a mess hall complete with cash drawers, lockable entrance and chairs. Each weekend I would bribe a fellow officer with my liquor ration to serve as my witnessing officer. We would sit for hours doling out pay and checking off names. When it got too noisy to work, I would stand up, wave my 45 pistol and yell "QUIET!" This usually worked. I hoped that in some way our visit there would be remembered favorably.

Big Problem Solved in a Big Way

Lest I leave the impression that my days as Labor Officer were all fun and games, I have to add a postscript. To accomodate the large number of laborers working in our camp, we dug regular G.I. latrines at the lower end of our camp. These facilities, complete with canvas walls and gravel floors were strictly for the use of those working in the camp area itself. To shorten travel time, many workers' family members resided in a large tent camp across a large brushy field behind the camp.

The fact that things had been going well for a while should have made me nervous. A bad signal came when a courier looked me up to inform me that I was to meet the head Medical Officer at the laborers latrines! My nerves reached the bursting point when the medical officer said something like "Lieutenant, what the hell is this?" He was referring to the piles of human feces liberally distributed in the gravel and also on the seat area. Who might have an answer to that query? "And this isn't all by a long shot," he shouted.. "Come with me!" We walked behind camp to the edge of the field of high grass and brush. "Take a big sniff," he instructed. I did so and immediately felt the need for a gas mask for the first time since our tear-gas training. Closer (and careful) examination showed the entire field to be literally "mined" with human waste. The enormity of it, and the ridiculous situation it presented must have finally come across as humorous, because I was never court-martialed or even officially reprimanded for failure to enforce proper standards of health.

The cure for all this began the next day when several road scrapers pushed all grass, brush and surface matter to the far end of the field. Trucks then dumped used motor oil from the motor pool on almost every foot of the field and ignited it! The smell hung heavy over the area for about three days.

I probably need not tell about my meeting with the head man, but I can report that a medical disaster was avoided, and never occurred again before the happy day I boarded that old tub that brought me back under the Golden Gate Bridge

Blackhawks Salute Our Flag

86th Blackhawks Salute Our Flag. Left to right: Bob Rasmus, "Red" Goodrich, Gene Lowe and soldier Paul Goodrich (Austin's grandson).

At the United Center in Chicago on Memorial Day 2007, a delegation of our Blackhawk Association participated in the flag-raising ceremony before a match between the Chicago Blackhawks and their National Hockey League arch rivals, the Detroit Red Wings. Pictured from left to Right are Bob Rasmus, Austin Goodrich, Gene Lowe and Army Reservist Paul Goodrich, Austin's grandson. The original owner of the hockey team, Major Frederick McLaughlin, named his team after the 86th Blackhawk Division with which he served in World War I. The fans gave us a standing ovation and our namesake team won the match 3–2!

Mindanao Mission
by Austin "Red" Goodrich 342nd K Co.

Some months after we set up our tent camp in Marakina, about an hour's donkey ride north of Manila, we were informed by our 3rd Battalion commander, Lt. Col. Ward, that we had been chosen to pack up and move to Mindanao at the southern end of the Philippine Islands chain. None of us knew anything about the place except that the Dole company raised and canned a bunch of pineapples there, and it was where the Colt .45 caliber automatic pistol proved its worth as the only weapon that could stop a crazed Moro tribesman in his tracks. Maj. Ward made it sound like it was an honor to be chosen for the assignment. And it did sound rather interesting. In any case it couldn't be less exhilarating than the garrison duty we were assigned to carry out on Luzon, where the only excitement was provided by throwing lighted firecrackers at the dancing feet of an unpopular sergeant's pet monkey.

So off we sailed to the second largest of the Philippine Islands where we set about erecting a second tent city. Fortunately, the setting was far above sea level, which meant that the place was considerably cooler and less humid than our camp on Luzon. Our specific assignment remained a mystery, but we assumed that it had something to do with manning road blocs on what appeared to be the only road on the island. We stopped and searched all who used this road though we weren't too clear on what exactly we were supposed to be looking for. Rumor had it that there were American troops on the island who were more or less running wild after most of there officers and non-coms had left for home to be discharged under the convoluted service points system. Another rumor had it that we were sent there to safeguard the property of the Dole company against theft and destruction by wild Moro tribesmen. Whatever our duties were, it was tacitly agreed by all that we would not permit official tasks assigned by the Army to interfere with our primary job of playing softball.

In this area, Company K had the advantage of owning a pitcher who was simply unhittable. Whenever this Mexican-American product of the Los Angeles semi-pro softball league took the mound, he played catch with the catcher while the seven other players on the team sat around at their positions, maybe munched a Baby Ruth candy bar or drank a bottle of Pabst beer. The opposing batters from other companies soon realized that their best and only hope was to choke halfway up on the bat, close their eyes and swing in the general area of the incoming pitch in hopes of making contact.

When darkness ended the hapless efforts attempts of our opponents to hit our ace, we repaired to our tents to light candles and get into our other island pastime—stud poker. The number of players gradually dropped as some of the sportsmen found other more satisfying outlets for their off duty energies. The women, some of whom came around to collect our laundry, and others who just happened to be attracted by our candlelight, were an attractive lot. The exotic features of the Orient blended nicely in the Filipina with a touch of familiar Caucasian bloodlines, and communication was facilitated by the fact that most of these women had been exposed to at least a smattering of English language instruction in their first grades in school.

The Filipina's exposure to western legal customs also clothed these arrangements with certain symbolic trappings of legality. It was considered necessary for the G.I. to provide his bride with a ring if he expected to enjoy her nocturnal favors. Generally, this requirement was satisfied by the comrade giving the girl friend his initialed high school class ring. I recall one instance, however, when a comrade had no class ring to offer and he desperately sought to get any sort of a ring. He knew of how another guy had sealed his bond with a local bride with a cigar ring, and he searched all over the place to find a comrade who could provide one. As fate would have it, all of us in the platoon either smoked cigarettes or didn't smoke at all. Finally the suitor was able to find a cigar-smoker in a neighboring tent who proved willing—at a price no doubt—to give him a cigar wrapper ring.

After several months of our Mindanao "service," we were summoned to an open-air battalion meeting called by Lt. Col. Ward. He prefaced his remarks by saying that he had some good news and some bad news. The good news was that we could all strike our tents and return to Luzon where we could wait for the time when our accumulation of points and the availability of ship would enable us to return home and become civilians. [thunderous applause]. But then came the bad news.

"Unfortunately," our commander continued, "the ship that's coming to port in two days does not pass the minimum requirements for the transportation of all our troops [massive boos and whistles]. "So I'll have to put this on a voluntary basis. You can vote to accept the sub-standard accommodations on the ship that's available or wait until a bigger ship comes into port. But I have to warn you that we don't have any idea how long we'll have to wait for another ship to come in here." After waiting for his message to sink in, our chief called for a vote, which was won by a unanimous agreement to accept sub-standard accommodations rather than waiting indefinitely for a ship that might never arrive.

Our sub-standard ship turned out to be an LST (Landing Ship Tanks) that had only a few officers-only cabins but ample open deck space. Using my full field pack as a pillow I lay down on a narrow steel walkway above the open deck now filled with men instead of tanks. After a few minutes it became apparent why these ships were never used to transport the weapons or personnel of war in the open sea. They were purposefully designed with a flat shallow bottom to disgorge tanks onto beachheads. We were never out of sight of land as our ungainly vessel gently rolled along its northward course through a maze of tiny islands under a sky free of pollution and filled with tiny, sparkling diamonds. And I thought what a beautiful curtain to draw across the final act of our war.

How I Nearly Became the Main Course
by "Red" Goodrich, 342nd K Co.

In Batangas, where we had landed on the southern shore of Luzon a few months before, I was on R&R with a platoon buddy. We had arranged to trade a mattress cover (which the local seamen used to patch the sails on their outriggers) for a two-day rental of one of their boats. We paddled this vessel around in the harbor until we reached the side of an old, coastal rust bucket riding at anchor. We pulled up alongside and a couple of smiling Filipino crewmen invited us to come abroad. We were then asked if we could dive from the ship's lower deck into the shimmering blue-green waters below.

We did so and the crew applauded. Then we were asked if we could dive from the upper deck, and we performed this feat to the applause and laughter of a fast-growing audience of deckhands. Finally, our egos were stroked by an invitation, more like a dare, to dive into the harbor from the ship's bridge.

Our answer to this challenge, which reached the outer limits of our courage, produced tumultuous applause and cheers from the entire crew lining the gunwales. Our ego trip completed. I asked one of our audience to do what we had just done. "Yeah, now you do it,' said I. Ah, no sir," he responded through a toothy grin that spread from ear to ear.

"Why not?" I asked.

This produced thunderous laughter from all of our fans. "No, come on," I said, "what's the matter? Don't you dare?" This produced more laughter, which ended when I got angry at their rude manners and demanded that the crew do what we had done. Then the answer came: "Shawks," said the crew's spokesman as he swept his hand across the waters of Batangas harbor.

"Oh, *sharks*," I said, as I swallowed a lump of fear the size of a mango pit. Our seagoing hosts all nodded, chuckled and in unison, pointed to the water below and repeated a single word: "shawks."

The next day I saw an old man of the sea drag a huge shark up onto the beach to the applause of a large group of consumers. How he ever got that monster fish into that little outrigger I'll never know. But I do know that it became the main course of village dinners that evening and the fisherman would be paid for his heroic catch with papayas and mangoes harvested by his neighbors. They didn't have any cash money, none at all.

What they had instead was a communal bond of shared poverty. Sort of like love.

The Last Battle
by Harold Campbell, 341st Hqs Co. 2nd Bn

Note: Campbell got involved in our last WWII battle nearly five months after the war had officially ended.

I was temporarily assigned to a detachment of our battalion that was sent to Lubang Island to repatriate a troublesome group of Japanese holdouts. We were transported to the island in landing craft and marched to a staging area near where the Japanese were thought to be. On February 22, 1946, our detachment of about 30 officers and men together with a Filipino regiment attempted to repatriate these Japanese holdouts. I was assigned to Lt. Holland as his radioman and I carried a standard 40-pound backpack field radio for him. Figuring that was enough to lug around, I elected not to carry my M-1 rifle. We formed a skirmish line, moved across a field and tried to communicate in Japanese using portable loudspeakers. Leaflets in Japanese had also been scattered in earlier efforts to reach out to them to no avail. Concealed in the undergrowth, they suddenly attacked us with rifle fire and we fell back as we returned their fire with an ear-shattering roar. Unable to defend myself, I quickly shed the radio and ran for cover, praying that I wouldn't be shot by our own guys. As far as I know that 40 lb radio may still be there! I later learned that two Filipino soldiers and at least six Japanese were killed in this firefight. I can't say how long the whole affair lasted. At the time it seemed like forever.

That ended our efforts for the day. We remained on the island for a few more days and then returned to our camp at Marikina. According to the news articles that appeared later, efforts to repatriate the holdouts continued and most of the remaining Japanese on Lubang Island surrendered in April 1946 without a fight. The Japanese commanding officer, Lt. Hiroo Onoda, the last holdout, surrendered twenty-eight years later, in March 1974, and was welcomed home as a hero a generation after the war ended. He was no hero. His unit, which he claimed had been stationed on Lubang to harass the Americans until reinforcements arrived was responsible for terrorizing and killing many peaceful Filipino civilians. I may add that to this day, the Japanese government has turned a blind eye to their responsibility for this unit and the atrocities they committed during World War II.

A Necessary Detour
by Harland Hesselberg 86 Div Hqs G-3

I was loading equipment in Mannheim, Germany, when someone called out my name, came over to the truck and said he had a telegram for me. I told him I knew what it was. My brother, Blaine, a Marine Paratrooper attached to the Raiders, who went behind Japanese lines to blow up their ammo dumps, had been killed in action on Iwo Jima. [Fast forward.]

While we were in the Philippines, I requested a leave to go to Iwo Jimo to visit his cemetery. I was already in the replacement depot waiting shipment home. About 1:00 pm, I was awakened and told my request was approved. Do I still wish to go? I said "Yes," and a Jeep took me to the airport. I boarded a plane and about six hours later landed in Okinawa instead of Iwo. I was told there were no more direct flights to Iwo. I stayed overnight and hitched a ride to Yonabaru air base to look for a flight. It so happened there were some Navy men there warming up their C-47. I asked the pilot if they were going to Iwo and he said "yes, but this is a condemned plane" and I would have to fly at my own risk. (I said that if they were willing to take a chance I would too!) It was about a four-hour hour flight and about an hour from Iwo one engine began to act up. One of the crew did some tampering and we got it running smoothly again. I stayed a couple of days and visited my brother's grave site.

My orders were to proceed to Saipan. I hitched a plane to Guam, where I looked up my brother Vernell, who was stationed there in the Navy. I spent the night with him then got a plane to Saipan, with a short stopover in Tinian ... I then boarded a ship back to the States, took a train ride home to be discharged at Camp McCoy, Wisconsin, thus ending my military service.

978-0-595-49556-6
0-595-49556-7

www.ingramcontent.com/pod-product-compliance
Lightning Source LLC
LaVergne TN
LVHW091109201125
826075LV00006B/61